COLUMBIA RIVER

THE ASTORIA ODYSSEY

A PICTORIAL HISTORY OF LIFE ON THE COLUMBIA RIVER ESTUARY

BRYAN PENTTILA

FRANK AMATO PUBLICATIONS, INC.
PORTLAND, OREGON

ACKNOWLEDGEMENTS

The historical societies of Clatsop County, Oregon and Pacific County, Washington and their devoted body of authors who keep their quarterlies, *Cumtux* and *Sou'wester*, respectfully, full of thoroughly researched and well-written articles deserve the foremost thanks. Through the tireless effort of these societies and concerned local individuals, the precious and fleeting human experiences of life along the Lower Columbia River will be recorded and recounted for generations to come. In addition, the staff and volunteers at the Astor Public Library who spent countless hours cataloguing Astoria's historic newspapers deserve recognition and praise.

I must also extend my sincere gratitude to two true gentlemen, Lorne Wirkkala and Robert Michael Pyle. And, of course, the loving support of my family has seen me through both the highs and lows.

We wish to thank the staff of The Compleat Photographer, and Sara Church Meyer especially, in Astoria, Oregon for the use of these fine historic photographs and their care in preserving and allowing us to share them with you!

DEDICATION

To Dan Sisson, the consummate outdoorsman, whose passion for wilderness and history is infectious.

THE AUTHOR

Bryan Penttila is a native Pacific Northwesterner. Raised in the southwest Washington timber town of Naselle, he graduated with a B.A. in History from Eastern Washington University in 2001. Whether toting his camera or fishing rod, being outdoors is his delight, although he manages to find a few spare moments to write. Published in several historical quarterlies, this is Bryan's first book. He still lives and works in the Naselle area.

All inquiries should be addressed to:
Frank Amato Publications, Inc.
P.O. Box 82112, Portland, Oregon 97282
503.653.8108 • www.amatobooks.com

Book & Cover Design: Michael Henderson
Printed in Hong Kong
Softbound ISBN: 1-57188-302-9 • UPC: 0-81127-00136-1

10 9 8 7 6 5 4 3 2 1

Contents

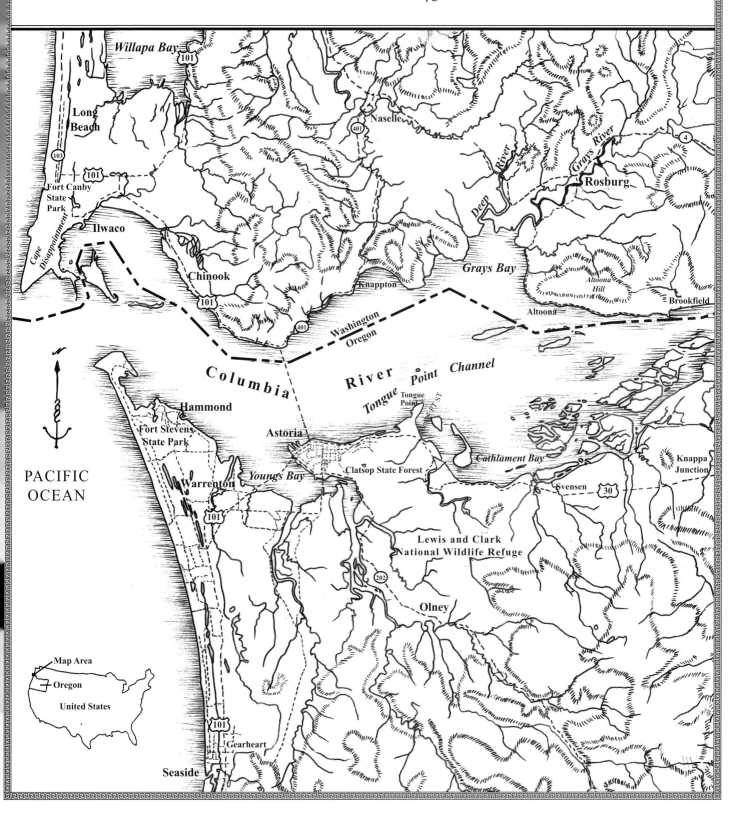

The Pacific Fur Company's fateful ship Tonquin *lays off Point George, surrounded by Indian canoes with Tongue Point gracing the skyline in the background.*

Ocian in View! O! The joy in Camp!" scribbled Captain William Clark in his leather-bound journal on the wet and blustery afternoon of November 7, 1805. Captain Clark, his co-commander Meriwether Lewis, and the twenty-nine members of their Corps of Discovery had trekked over four thousand miles to reach this point, the fulfillment of their western exploration. In their haste to see the long-awaited Pacific, the Corps had traveled some thirty-four miles down the Columbia River that day before pitching camp near Pillar Rock, a bastion of basalt jutting out of the river. That miserable day, as the captain cast his gaze westward to view the ocean breakers crashing into the river's mouth, he oversaw a broad sheet of water, the Columbia River Estuary.

After tumbling some eleven hundred miles out of the Canadian Rockies, sweeping through the Palouse sage lands, and cutting swiftly through its awe-inspiring gorge, the Columbia River crashes into the deep blue of the Pacific Ocean. As Captain Clark beheld this last great expanse of the Columbia he could hardly have imagined the scope of enterprise and commerce that would one day flourish along its heavily timbered banks. Indeed, this estuary would be, for a time, the hub of the Pacific Coast fur trade as well as home to the most renowned salmon fishery in the world. This tidal estuary would carry the ships full of grain and lumber to nourish peoples in myriad regions and build the economic structure for civilization along all reaches of the river.

❦

Thirteen years prior to the arrival of the Corps of Discovery, Captain Robert Gray, an American trader from Boston piloting the ship Columbia Rediviva, became the first skipper to guide his ship across the bar of the river to be named for his vessel. The Columbia Bar had long been sighted by both Spanish and British mariners, many of whom believed it to be little more than a broad inlet of minimal significance. British navigators had tried unsuccessfully to enter this treacherous waterway, naming its northern entrance Cape Disappointment to echo their sentiments. But, on May 11, 1792, only weeks after the most recent British attempt, Captain Gray crossed the bar and found safe anchorage and fresh water. As the *Columbia Rediviva*, a mere eighty-three feet in length, came to rest along the river's north shore a flotilla of Chinook Indian canoes rushed to greet the new arrivals.

Captain Gray graciously welcomed the Native Americans for they possessed the very articles he sought: sea otter furs. Since the 1778 voyage of British Captain James Cook, daring seafarers had trafficked in the highly lucrative sea otter pelts. The Pacific fur trade began with the collection of furs from Pacific Northwest Indian tribes which were shipped across the ocean to China. In China the furs were traded for silk, spices, tea, and porcelain, which were in turn sold in western markets for extraordinary prices. Gray, a relative late-comer to the Pacific fur trade, was rewarded handsomely for his boldness in crossing the Columbia Bar. The crew of the *Columbia Rediviva* vigorously engaged in trade with the Native Peoples collecting one hundred-fifty sea otter pelts as well as three hundred beaver skins. More of a practical man than an explorer, Gray ventured upriver only fifteen miles before leaving the newly christened Columbia River.

The Native inhabitants of the Lower Columbia River that Robert Gray first encountered on that fateful spring day in 1792 were a dynamic and vibrant people. They were the Lower Chinooks—four independent groups linked by a common language and culture: The Wahkiakums inhabiting much of what is now Wahkiakum County, Washington; the Cathlamets living along Cathlamet Bay on the Columbia River's south bank; the Clatsops who dwelt along the south bank of the river's mouth around Young's Bay; and the Shoalwater Chinook who occupied the north bank as far north as today's Willapa Bay.

The Chinookian people were short and brawny with dark, alert eyes, their narrow, high noses offset by a wide and expressive mouth. Their skin was lighter than that of most Native Americans as was their hair which possessed a reddish-brown hue. A common practice among free Chinooks was the flattening of the forehead. The deformation of the skull began when the newborn infant was tied in the cradleboard and a hinged cedar board laced firmly over the fore-

Bold seafarers have called upon the Columbia River since Robert Gray first crossed the bar in 1792.

head. As the child grew the forehead became elongated, emphasizing the facial features. The process lasted for as long as a year. The flattened forehead became an unequivocal sign of both beauty and freedom in traditional Chinook society. The process certainly did not harm the infant's brain for the Chinooks were noted by early fur traders and explorers for their intelligence and power of memory.

The Chinooks lived in long, rectangular homes built of split cedar planks and posts, some as long as ninety feet. Entire families dwelt in the same long house heated by a fire burning in the center of the floor. Inside these lodges, oral traditions were passed from elders to the young with exact retellings. The bonds between Chinook families proved to be an unyielding and critical facet of their culture.

They had a highly stratified societal structure. The four basic social classes were upper class, commoners, free persons, and slaves. Slavery was a common practice among north coast Indians. The slaves were either purchased or taken as spoils of victory in battles with enemy tribes. The Chinooks set their slaves about the routine tasks of hunting, fishing, wood chopping, and paddling. They were also used as means of barter and were given as gifts. Any free Chinook could own slaves but oftentimes only the upper class could afford them. Ten to twenty-five percent of the population of a Chinook village was held in bondage.[1] It was the slave's unfortunate duty to follow his or her master to the afterlife, being put to death and buried under the posts of the master's raised burial canoe.

Strategically located between inland tribes and those along the northern coast, the Chinooks were at the crossroads of a major trade network. They enjoyed wealth unknown to most North American Indians. Historians have labeled the Chinooks "the traders of the Columbia," whose waters carried a wide array of goods: arrowheads, baskets, beads, berries, canoes, furs, leathers, shells, salmon, slaves, wapato roots, whale oil and blubber. Trade items came from as far away as the southern Alaska coast, northern California, and the distant Rocky Mountains. Of all the tribes trafficking goods throughout the Northwest, the Chinooks were perhaps the most astute bargain makers. Contact with white traders only increased the Chinooks' wealth and business acumen.

Overseeing their trade monopoly was the wealthiest and most powerful Chinook of them all, the one-eyed Comcomly. This masterful trader had been a young man in his mid-twenties when Robert Gray first entered the Columbia, and ascended to a position of preeminence among the tribe in the succeeding years. Leadership positions were not bestowed by heredity but based on wealth, of which Comcomly could claim much. He took it upon himself to personally greet each incoming ship, lavishing the captain with numerous gifts, thereby winning the executive officer's admiration and favor. Comcomly, a well-built man with short, dark-brown hair, had four wives from surrounding tribes, effectively cementing solid political and trading allegiances.

⚓

Given their prior contact with white explorers, Comcomly and his fellow Chinooks seemed rather unsurprised when a ragged party of some thirty white men, a Plains Indian woman with her baby, and a black slave hove into view in November 1805. It was bizarre, however, that the white men came down the river rather than from the sea as they always had before, and word of their coming raced down river faster than Lewis and Clark's rough-hewn pine canoes could carry them. The first Americans to cross the continent were nearing the end of their western exploration. Only eighteen months before the Corps of Discovery had, a half continent away, set up the Missouri River at the behest of President

Thomas Jefferson in an attempt to chart with "great pains & accuracy" the most direct water route to the ocean and now on November 7, could see the white-capped waves crashing between the receding banks of the river. "Great joy in camp we are in View of the Ocian, this great Pacific Octean which we been So long anxious to See," wrote William Clark. The Corps' exuberance was muffled, however, by the incessant

Visiting delegates from both the Nez Perce and Yakima tribes joined descendents of the Clatsop and Shoalwater Chinook to represent the Pacific Northwest's Native American population at the centennial celebration.

rains. The following morning dawned blustery and wet as the party set out toward the ocean, skirting the river's north shore. Hampered by a savage storm and ripping tides, the Lewis and Clark expedition could make little westward progress, not rounding Point Ellice as a group until November 15. Both Lewis and Clark took turns reconnoitering Cape Disappointment and the south Long Beach

Right: Noted Pacific Northwest photographer Ashel Curtis captured this cheerless image of a Native American woman collecting drift wood in 1910.

Chinook Indian boats were often very long to accommodate a large passenger count. This photograph was taken just upstream of the Columbia River Gorge near The Dalles, Oregon, about 200 miles upstream from Astoria.

FORT CLATSOP 1805·06 WINTER QUARTERS of LEWIS and CLARK EXPEDITION

The Corps of Discovery spent the dreary winter of 1806 at Fort Clatsop, a log bastion they constructed on the banks of the Lewis and Clark River.

Peninsula hoping to find an outpost of white traders rumored to reside there. No trading post was located, but a grove of trees on Baker's Bay was found with the names of numerous ships and sailors scribed on them. Lewis carved on one tree "By Land from the U. States in 1804 & 1805."

Where to spend the winter soon became an issue. There were three choices at hand: to proceed back upriver and winter at the falls, to stay among the Chinooks, or cross to the south bank (where Lewis and Clark were told game was plentiful) and examine the other shore before deciding. A democratic vote was held—the first of its kind in the Pacific Northwest—where all cast their opinion, including the female Indian interpreter Sacagawea and slave York. With only one dissenting vote, the decision to explore the possibilities of the south shore won. After a harrowing and delay-plagued crossing, Lewis found a suitable site for the construction of a fort. Hampered by disagreeable weather from the outset, work commenced December 7. The diminutive stockade, named Fort Clatsop in honor of the local Indians, was completed five days after Christmas.

Fort life quickly settled into a cheerless routine. A salt-making station was located at modern-day Seaside and crews set to work boiling sea water to collect the precious preservative. The Corps' diet consisted almost exclusively of boiled and smoked venison, mostly elk meat. Breaking the drudgery were regular visits by local Indians interested in trading goods and sexual favors. As a result of the wretched coastal weather, poor diet, and sexual liaisons with Indian women, the men at Fort Clatsop were often sick with colds, the flu, and venereal disease. One of Lewis and Clark's favorite visitors during the winter of 1806 was the Clatsop chief Coboway, who they considered "the most friendly and decent savage that we have met with in this neighborhood." So after the dreary winter at Fort Clatsop collecting zoological, botanical, and ethnographic information for President Jefferson, the Corps of Discovery left Fort Clatsop March 22, 1806, returning safely to St. Louis the following September after being gone for two years and five months. Besides returning with a wealth of observations regarding natural science, the Corps of Discovery had mapped the unknown void between the Missouri and the Pacific Ocean, making the West something the American mind could deal with more easily.

❧

From the time of Lewis and Clark's departure from Fort Clatsop in 1806 until 1810 the Chinooks reigned as the preeminent traders along the big river. The tribe held power as the middlemen between the region's tribes and white traders. After wintering in the Sandwich Islands, today's Hawaii, trading vessels would enter the river in April and continue trading generally until October. The Chinooks would recognize a ship and know its master's name and trading adroitness. Trading would commence, both sides being well rewarded. After collecting furs for two seasons (1808-1809) and some sandalwood in Hawaii, one Boston ship returned to New England with a gross profit in excess of $200,000, a four hundred percent return for the investors.[2]

The Chinooks' power was again asserted in the summer of 1810 with the arrival of the Boston ship *Albatross*. Onboard were twenty-four hearty young New Englanders and a troop of Hawaiians sent west by the Winship brothers, Boston men well-versed in the Pacific fur trade. Their mission was to establish a fur emporium along the banks of the Columbia. The little vessel ascended the river, sounding the channel as they went, and after about fifty miles an attractive oak grove came into view. On the south bank, near today's Clatskanie, Oregon, a low, level opening was selected and all hands went to work clearing ground for a garden and a fortified bastion. By the following day a suitable garden had been planted and the hewed timbers began to resemble a fortification.

Unfortunately for the Winships, there were two steadfast aspects of life along the Columbia they had overlooked. The first element was rain. The downpour, combined with summer snowmelt from far away mountains, served to swell the river engulfing the garden and the partially constructed walls. The master of the *Albatross*, Nathan Winship, ordered the fort disassembled and floated to higher ground. Just then the second oversight arrived—canoes full of them. It was the Chinooks, and they were livid. To establish a trading post so far upriver would directly threaten their trading empire. Already uneasy, the *Albatross'* crew continued to float the timbers until the agitated Indians began to whoop and fire shots into the air. Work ceased immediately and all hands returned to the ship posthaste.

A canoe full of Chinook dignitaries, including Comcomly, paddled alongside the *Albatross*, relating to the Winships they did not mind the construction of the fort only its location. They persuaded the men from Boston to relocate, farther down the river. The sailors followed the Chinook flotilla to Baker's Bay and commenced trading furs. Unable to carry out their plan, the Winships opted to give up on their ambitious project. One of the Winships' assistants noted of the Chinooks, "The country was theirs." And so, the first "permanent" American establishment along the Columbia lasted only eight days. But, the following spring a more earnest and well-funded undertaking would be launched at Point George, near the river's mouth, taking the name Astoria.

❧

The concept for Astoria's founding came from the mind of John Jacob Astor, a German immigrant and one of America's preeminent fur traders. By the turn of the nineteenth century, Astor saw the massive potential for Northwest furs traded to China. He began by purchasing cargo space on ships bound for China. The returns were incredible. By 1807, Astor conceived a string of fur-trading posts up the Missouri River, over the Rocky Mountains, and along the Columbia River with direct access to Chinese markets. His fur emporium at the mouth of the Columbia River would be his Pacific Coast headquarters.

Astor sought out the most able men from competing fur companies to bring his dream to fruition. Canadian traders Alexander McKay and Duncan McDougall were hired to sail around Cape Horn and establish the trading post while an American, Wilson Price Hunt, agreed to lead an overland party to the mouth of the Columbia with Canadian Donald McKenzie his second in command. On June 23, 1810 the Pacific Fur Company was incorporated with Astor pledging up to a maximum of $400,000 and controlling one-half of the shares. He had eight partners in the enterprise—including McKay, McKenzie, McDougall, and Hunt—who each received a certain number of shares to ensure loyalty and motivation. Astor purchased a sturdy ship named the

Tonquin and put at its helm Jonathan Thorn, a capable United States navy lieutenant on official leave. On September 6, 1810, the *Tonquin*, with a diversified cargo featuring everything from colored cloth to nearly a ton of gun powder, left New York harbor and sailed into history.

The *Tonquin* reached the Pacific Ocean after an uneventful voyage. Thorn's inflexible and peevish character led to several scuffles and had served to polarize all onboard. Upon reaching the Columbia River bar, eight men were lost when Captain Thorn ordered smaller boats launched to sound for passable channels. Despite the tragic loss, the *Tonquin* safely crossed the bar and found safe harbor in the river April 11, 1811.

While scouting potential sites for the trading house, Duncan McDougall's boat capsized in the heavy swells, sending the trader and his comrades into the river. The vigilant Comcomly, casually trailing the Astorians in his large canoe, pressed his rowers forward and saved the distressed men. After feeding and warming the waterlogged traders in his village, the tribal leader returned them to the *Tonquin*, setting in motion a trusting and peaceful association.

The search for suitable sites was renewed immediately. A rolling hill on the Columbia River's south bank, Point George, was selected as the most satisfactory site for the station. The site did not wholly satisfy the traders but Captain Thorn's haste to continue his trading mission up the coast dictated the settlement's location. In his rush, Thorn left the Columbia before fully unloading all the supplies, leaving the pioneers to fend for themselves. Construction of the fortification proceeded at once. The partners decided to name the establishment Fort "Astoria" in honor of its patriarch John Jacob Astor.

Meanwhile, the overland party had left Montreal in the summer of 1810, picking up American and Canadian trappers as it headed toward St. Louis. Led by Wilson Price Hunt and Donald McKenzie, the overland expedition started up the Missouri River in October 1810. After wintering along the banks of the Missouri, the expedition, consisting of nearly fifty men, set out the following April with plans to follow the trail pioneered by Lewis and Clark. Rumors of hostile Indians on the upper reaches of the Missouri River convinced Hunt to disobey Astor's orders and leave the established route, favoring a more southerly path instead. The results were deadly. After losing their way, the overland party suffered thirst, hunger, sickness, and a number of deaths before reaching the Snake River. It was not until January 19, 1812 that the first part of Hunt's overland expedition reached the Columbia and after a rapid descent of the river landed at Astoria on February 15.

On May 5, 1812 a third detachment of Astorians arrived on the Columbia River aboard Astor's ship Beaver. The ship also carried the news of the destruction of the *Tonquin*. The Astorians had heard a rumor from the local Indians that the

Tonquin had been destroyed while on her trading mission but vested little faith in it. Indeed, after leaving the Columbia, the *Tonquin* sailed north trading along the coast as ordered. Off Vancouver Island, Captain Thorn outraged an Indian chief by rubbing an inferior pelt in his face when a satisfactory price could not be agreed upon. Thorn's impetuous action led the Indians to overrun the ship in an act of retribution the following morning. Only one sailor survived the initial slaughter to slip below decks and ignite nearly a ton of gun powder remaining in the hold, obliterating the *Tonquin* and everyone onboard.

Despite the long series of tragedies, life at the newly constructed outpost of Astoria settled into a familiar routine. The rollicking adventures recounted by later chroniclers seem to have overlooked the doldrums of daily affairs. The trappers, traders, carpenters, cooks, clerks, laborers, and blacksmith went about their tasks day after day. The most common phrase in Astoria's official log kept by Duncan McDougal is "people employed as usual."

In order to guard their trading monopoly, the Chinooks utilized deceit with both the Astorians and surrounding Indians. The Chinooks convinced local tribes that the new arrivals were monstrous cannibals, while telling the traders that the competing tribes were brutish savages.[3] All seemed to be going well for the Chinooks. Nearby Indians paid the Chinooks a steep markup to risk bringing pelts to the fort, while the Astorians paid an additional markup to buy from the only hospitable tribe around. Astor had sent his men to take advantage of these supposedly primitive people but were in turn being swindled. Before long, however, the Pacific Fur partners caught on to the scheme and were openly irritated. Found at fault, the Chinooks reluctantly accepted the traders' prices and normal trading relations commenced. To ensure continued relations, Comcomly gave his daughter Illchee's hand in marriage to Duncan McDougall in July 1813. The Astorian in turn bestowed the headman with an impressive stock of guns, blankets, and beads. The ceremony and following celebration took place outside the fort's gate. Comcomly utilized his new connection, visiting the fort regularly—oftentimes calling upon the company blacksmith for metal trinkets. In 1823, another of Comcomly's daughters wed a Hudson's Bay Company clerk, establishing ties with British traders.

Astor's vision of a string of interior forts slowly became a reality. The Astorians built Fort Okanogan, the first American structure in what would become Washington State. They later built Fort Spokane and established trading posts on the Clearwater and Boise rivers. But, just as the Astorians' prospects looked brightest, international affairs intervened.

On June 18, 1812, Congress declared war on Great Britain, the ramifications of which would directly affect Astoria. Partner Donald McKenzie reached Astoria in

ASTORIA 1855

O.B. Este
1900

Astoria's first wharf completed in the early 1850s.

January 1813 with word from an inland trading post that the United States and Great Britain were at war and relayed a rumor that the British ship *Isaac Todd* was en route to the Columbia to capture the outpost. Because most of the employees at Astoria were Canadians trading under the American flag, loyalties would be mixed. Realizing the British would have eastern ports blockaded, the partners held a council of war where they weighed their situation. Without telling the men, the partners decided to make plans to abandon the fort the following spring or early summer. With no idea how long it would be before the *Isaac Todd* arrived at Astoria, work on a detailed inventory began and progress on trading affairs hurried.

In early October 1813 a flotilla of ten canoes from the British-owned North West Company rounded Tongue Point, a peninsula jutting out into the Columbia from the south shore, and landed at Astoria. They had come to await the arrival of the *Isaac Todd*. The partners at Astoria soon entered into crucial negotiations with North West Company officials. Under duress, with all options exhausted, Duncan McDougall agreed to sell Astoria along with all of its provisions and arms October 16, 1813.

It was not the *Isaac Todd* but a faster sloop-of-war, Racoon, that crossed the bar to capture the Pacific Fur Company's headquarters at Astoria. Astoria's first and only conqueror, British Captain William Black, saw humor in the crudely assembled fort's physical insignificance. Determined to carry out his orders despite the official sale of Astoria two months earlier, Black went ashore and oversaw the formal surrender of Fort Astoria on the afternoon of December 12, 1813. The Union Jack was hoisted and Astoria became a wartime prize of Great Britain.

Captain Black left Astoria in the hands of the North West Company, who renamed it Fort George. Back in New York, John Jacob Astor did not get word of his loss until the fall of 1814. Astor was fifty-one years old when the Treaty of Ghent was signed on Christmas Eve, 1814, ending the War of 1812. One article in the treaty stipulated that all lands captured during the conflict would be returned to the country with previous title. No one knew what to do with Astoria—Astor claimed Captain Black had "captured" his fort; the North West Company held that the outpost was legally purchased before Black ever arrived on the Columbia. With his Columbia River monopoly ruined, Astor chose not to pursue his ambitious western plans and instead shifted his focus back to the Missouri River.

In April 1814 the supply ship Isaac Todd finally arrived in Astoria. None of its cargo excited more interest than a blonde-haired, blue-eyed English barmaid named Jane Barnes. Astoria's first white woman, the mistress of a North West Company official, caught the fancy of Comcomly's eldest son Chenamus. Smitten, he offered Ms. Barnes a hundred sea otter skins, a life of leisure, and superiority over his other wives to become his bride. The nature of her refusal went unrecorded, but undoubtedly Chenamus was let down after such a lavish offer. Jane Barnes left Fort George shortly thereafter and wed a British sea captain, returning to visit the fort a few years later.

In 1818, a joint-occupation treaty was signed giving both the United States and Great Britain equal claims to the Pacific Northwest.

Three years later the Hudson's Bay Company absorbed the North West Company and under factor George Simpson moved the headquarters some ninety miles up the Columbia River to Fort Vancouver in 1824. Astoria was left virtually deserted. The relocation by Hudson's Bay marked a collapse of the Chinook people.

The Chinooks had endured European epidemics before, but the removal of their nearby trading post coincided with one of the worst scourges they had ever endured. Smallpox, likely carried over the Rocky Mountains, swept through their ranks as early as 1781, leaving survivors pock-scarred and some even blind. After ships began calling on the Columbia, syphilis and gonorrhea contracted from sailors ran rampant. But the "fever" of 1824-25 and 1830 proved the most deadly. Entire villages were wiped out. Unattended corpses littered the beaches and decimated villages. Even the great Comcomly succumbed to the pestilence in 1830. Dr. John McLouglin, superintendent of Fort Vancouver, estimated seventy-five percent of the remaining Indians between the Cascades and the ocean perished.[4] The scattered and broken peoples that remained left their villages that they considered cursed, many assimilating into European settlements.

Astoria, or Fort George, began a rapid descent. The Hudson's Bay Company retained only two employees at the old outpost and gave up on improving the facility. The soggy climate began taking its toll on the fort that the Astorians had labored to construct. By the late 1830s and early 1840s, Astoria had but one European resident—a listless Scot trader employed by the Hudson's Bay Company named James Birnie. His outpost, although still referred to as Fort George, no longer had a stockade, a bastion, nor anything associated with a fortification. It was a simple hewed log cabin surrounded by Indian longhouses. A lone crumbling chimney remained as the last vestige of the Fort Astoria of 1811.[5]

❦

Although Astor's bold decision to establish a trading post in foreign territory solely inhabited by Native Americans at the far edge of the continent lasted less than two years it struck a romantic chord with the nation. Astoria had epitomized the young republic's desire for adventure and expansion, dubbed by New York newspaperman John Louis O'Sullivan "Manifest Destiny." It embodied the country's romantic western ideals of courage, fortitude, and daring. The name "Astoria" was soon being trumpeted in expansionist speeches on the floor of the United States Senate. People began equating the venture's boldness with its greatness, creating a mystique Astoria could not live up to.

Astoria's notoriety was only enhanced with the release, in the fall of 1836, of Washington Irving's book *Astoria, or Anecdotes of an Enterprise Beyond the Rocky Mountains*. Several years prior to Irving's book, two of the clerks from the original Astoria expedition published their notes raising questions regarding Astor's role in Fort Astoria's failure. In response, Astor approached Irving, one the America's most eminent writers, to tell his side of the story thereby ensuring his lasting reputation as a true patriot and visionary. Irving was paid a handsome stipend. The monograph sold remarkably well and further increased Astoria's standing as an American icon.

Visitors to Astoria in the 1830s and 1840s were less than impressed with the establishment's appearance however. Lieutenant Charles Wilkes, the leader of the United States Exploring Expedition, found the "somewhat famous" village to be "any thing but what I should wish to describe." He surmised, "Half of a dozen log houses, with as many sheds and a pig-sty or two are all that it can boast of." Another journal keeper described Astoria as a mostly overgrown "thicket of spruce and briars," with "Five or six old dilapidated buildings, which are occupied by the Hudson's Bay Company." Even the future president Ulysses Grant, a second lieutenant in the army at the time, concluded his 1852 observations of "Astoria—a place that we see on maps, and read about," with the disillusioned phrase "So much for Astoria."

❧

In 1844, James K. Polk was elected president of the United States on an expansionist platform calling, in part, to re-occupy Oregon. The provocative cry of "Fifty-four Forty or Fight" rang across the nation. Nevertheless, in 1846 the United States and Britain agreed to draw the international boundary along the 49th parallel. As America realized the northwest corner of its "Manifest Destiny," prospective settlers began to look west. Since Dr. Elijah White's great wagon train of nearly one hundred settlers arrived in Willamette Valley in the fall of 1842, the volume of overland emigrants had steadily increased. Although a large portion of the Oregon-bound pioneers took up claims in the Willamette Valley some looked farther west and saw potential in the dormant village of Astoria.

In 1843, one such immigrant, J.M. Shively, settled there. After establishing a home site near the original fort, Shively departed for the East Coast, returning in 1847 with a commission as a postmaster. That year in Astoria he established the first United States post office west of the Rocky Mountains—Portland would not have a post office for another two years. Mail from Astoria's regional distributing center was dispersed throughout what was to become Oregon, Washington, Idaho, and Montana.

The next significant event in Astoria's history was the arrival of a tall, lean Kentuckian with a commanding presence, sent west by President Polk. John Adair, the first Collector-General of Customs for the Oregon District, arrived by way of the Pacific April 4, 1849 to establish a customs house at Astoria. Besides collecting duties from cargos transported in and out of the river, the customs house affirmed American sovereignty over the greater Columbia region. The structure itself was erected in east Astoria, or Uppertown, across Scow Bay from the old fort and the heart of Astoria's settlement—creating a riff that would later cause a municipal dilemma. Nevertheless, the founding of the customs house could not have been more timely.

An 1848 discovery along the boulder-strewn banks of California's American River would soon change Astoria's fortune forever: gold, the allure of which was to bring tens of thousands of 49ers to Northern California and open new markets for entrepreneurs throughout the newly created Oregon Territory. Only months after the gold strike, the United States Congress forged the boundaries of the territory, encompassing approximately 350,000 square miles, which would later be split up into the states of Oregon, Washington, and Idaho. Still, the lion's share of passengers, mail, and cargo transported through the territory was shipped on the waters of the Columbia River.

❧

The sands and sediments of a watershed encompassing over a quarter of a million square miles accumulate near the Columbia's mouth as they filter into the abyssal Pacific Ocean, creating the most savage and unpredictable bar on the northwest coast. The incessant surf rolls across the ever-shifting sands of the river's five-mile-wide mouth. Lieutenant Charles Wilkes preformed the first official American survey of the Columbia Bar in 1841. "Mere description can give little idea of the terrors of the bar of the Columbia…" reported Wilkes. He declared the bar to be "…one of the most fearful sights that can possibly meet the eye of the sailor." It was during Wilkes' original survey that one of his ships, the brig Peacock, was lost, lending its name to its final resting place, the long spit at the river's north entrance.

With the increased ship traffic spurred by the Gold Rush the rate of accidents increased. These turbulent waters soon earned the nickname "The Graveyard of the Pacific." Four major wrecks occurred in 1849 and five in 1852, claiming sixty-one lives. Even before the Gold Rush, in 1847, bar pilot licenses were issued to Captains Hustler, Reeves, and White for their commanding knowledge of the river's mouth. The bar pilots boarded inbound vessels via the sixty-foot pilot schooner *Mary Taylor* while still in the ocean, commanding the ships through the restless bar and disembarking at Astoria. Similarly, outbound ships were boarded at Astoria, guided across the bar, and the pilots returned on the *Mary Taylor*.

One of the earliest and most extraordinary bar pilots was Captain George Flavel. Born of Irish parentage, Flavel was a twenty-five-year-old captain when his ship reached the gold-crazed San Francisco harbor in 1849. In short order he became master of a coasting vessel running between the Columbia River and San Francisco. On September 22, 1850 he received his branch license as a bar pilot for the Territory of Oregon. Flavel formed an early bar pilots' association and purchased a sixty-four-foot pilot boat, the schooner California. Flavel charged high rates but provided excellent service, maintaining a near monopoly on Columbia Bar piloting for nearly two decades.

Flavel's courage was tested from the start. In January 1852, he successfully guided the steam-powered sailing vessel General Warren to sea. Loaded to the hilt with hogs, wheat, and fifty-two passengers, the San Francisco-bound ship encountered a strong gale, knocking the fore-topmast down and springing a leak. The water-soaked grain choked the pumps, convincing the ship's master he should return to Astoria for repairs. She was sighted by the California the following afternoon and Flavel brought back onboard. With grave reluctance, Flavel attempted to bring the General Warren across the bar at the urging of the captain and passengers. Fighting the ebb tide on steam-power alone the ship could make no headway. The decision to ground the vessel was made. As darkness descended it began to snow, and the General Warren's course change sent the floundering ship onto Clatsop Spit, striking the sand bar with a terrific impact. Flavel and ten volunteers boarded the only lifeboat not ravaged by the storm, and set off for Astoria. He shouted to the captain: "If I live, I will return." Riding the change of tide the boat made the snow-swirling voyage in remarkable time—some three hours. At Astoria two large whaleboats were provisioned and the new crews set forth to rescue the General Warren's survivors. When they reached the spot of the grounding nothing remained. The crashing surf had disintegrated the vessel; nothing was visible. Forty-two dead bodies were eventually recovered, including a newlywed couple locked in an eternal embrace. For his indomitable bravery, the citizens of Portland presented Flavel a gold medal, but more importantly he won the trust and admiration of sea captains all along the Pacific Coast.

❦

The city of Astoria was incorporated by the Oregon Territorial legislature on January 18, 1856. The town consisted of a wharf, constructed in the early fifties, and several dozen houses. The public buildings included a schoolhouse, a Methodist Church, and, of course, the post office and customs house.

Although there are no official census returns for Astoria in 1860, the population probably numbered about two hundred and fifty souls.[6] Continued growth was sustained by the erection of nearby Forts Stevens and Canby at the river's mouth during the Civil War. To aid shipping, a lighthouse was completed atop Cape Disappointment in 1856, two hundred and twenty feet above the Columbia. Its rotating light, the first permanent one in the Pacific Northwest, generated an unmistakable beacon for weary seafarers.

Simultaneous with Astoria's growth and improved shipping, settlers began taking land claims on the north bank in and around the sites of vacant Chinook Indian villages. Chinookville, located just west of Point Ellice, was probably the first European settlement in what would become Pacific County, Washington. Later, in 1853, with the creation of the Washington Territory, Chinookville was elected that county's first seat of government. The location had previously been home to a sizeable and thriving Chinook Indian village, upwards of four hundred inhabitants in all. During the 1830s, Catholic missionaries, including well-known clerics Francis Norbert Blanchet and Pierre Jean De Smet, a Jesuit missionary, visited Chinookville. In addition, Methodist preacher Daniel Lee, nephew to Jason Lee, held services on occasion at the Chinook village. In 1840 the Hudson's Bay Company erected a store at Chinookville giving rise, by the 1850s, to a sleepy village of fishermen, seafarers, and merchants.

The land encompassing Chinookville had long been the traditional salmon fishing-grounds for the Lower Chinook Indians. From time immemorial, five species of Pacific salmon had swum past this expanse of sandy beach. The anadromous salmon—born in fresh water, living three to five years in the ocean, traveling thousands of miles, before returning to the Columbia and its tributaries from spring until the fall to spawn and die—provided the Native Peoples with a major food source and trading commodity. As with the region's Indians, the newly arrived settlers utilized the bountiful runs of salmon. In the 1830s, the Hudson's Bay Company established salmon salting stations along the north bank during salmon season.

Seining was the most common method of harvesting the fish. James Swan, an early ethnographer and journal keeper, witnessed the salmon-fishing spectacle near Chinookville in the early 1850s. He noted: "Three persons are required to work a net, except the very large ones, which require more help to land them. The time the fishing is commenced is at the top of high-water, just as the tide begins to ebb. A short distance from the shore the current is very swift, and with its aid these nets are hauled. Two persons get into the canoe, on the stern of which is coiled the net on a frame made for the

Right: Some Astorians viewed the Pacific Northwest as the neck of a funnel that was the Columbia River. With its deep-water port, proximity to the ocean, and abundance of natural resources like timber and salmon, many settlers believed Astoria to be the future commercial capital of the Pacific Northwest .

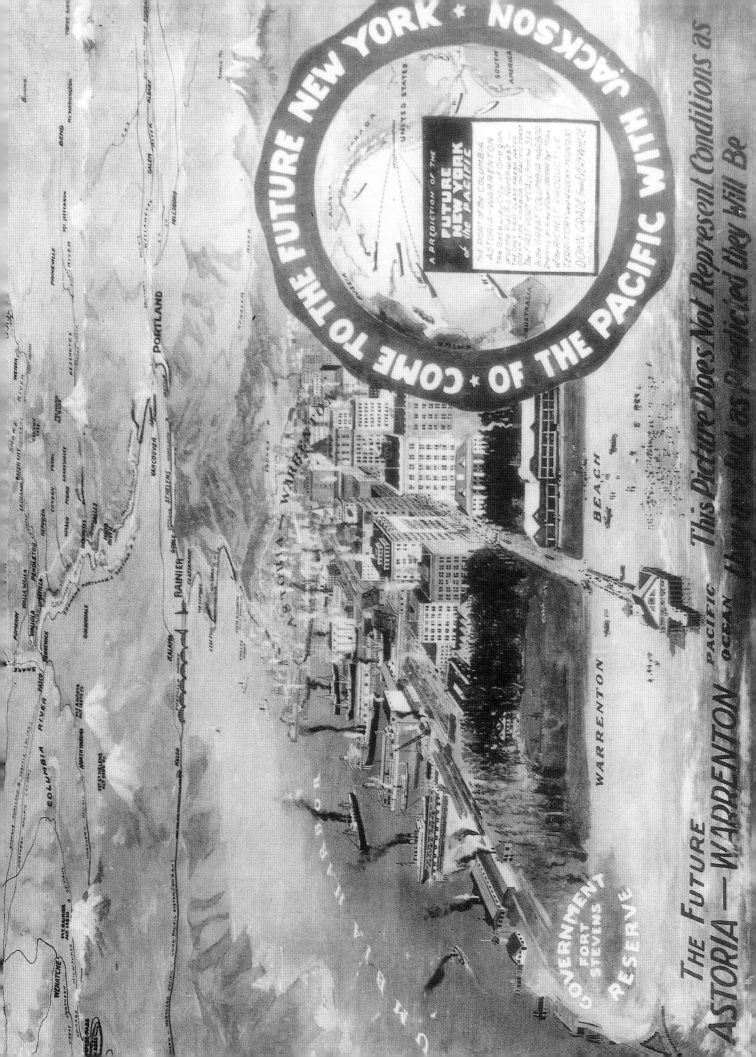

Gillnetters of the "butterfly fleet," aptly named for the graceful curvature of their sails, ply the water for salmon in front of Astoria prior to the turn of the twentieth century. The sail-driven double-ender gillnet boats were all but obsolete by the 1920s.

purpose, resting on the canoe's gunwale. She is then paddled up the stream, close in to the beach, where the current is not so strong. A tow-line, with a wooden float attached to it, is then thrown to the third person, who remains on the beach, and immediately the two in the canoe paddle her into the rapid stream as quickly as they can, throwing out the net all the time. When this is all out, they paddle ashore, having the end of the other tow-line made fast to the canoe. Before all this is accomplished, the net is carried down the stream, by the force of the ebb, about the eighth of a mile, the man on the shore walking along slowly, holding on to the line till the others are ready, when all haul together."[7]

Once closed and the fish ensnared the net was hauled ashore. Swan related that a good haul of the seine would produce one hundred salmon of various sizes. In the early summer, fish of eighty pounds were not uncommon. Swan talked to one Chinook resident who had twelve fish in his smoke house averaging sixty-five pounds, the largest of which weighed seventy-eight pounds. Throughout the 1850s and much of the 1860s, smoking and salting remained the surest way to preserve salmon. That is until the year 1866.

After founding the California salmon canning industry in 1864, the illustrious Hume brothers—William, George, Joseph, and Robert—began operations on the Columbia River in 1866. Along with tinsmith Andrew Hapgood, the Humes built a cannery in eastern Wahkiakum County at a spot they designated Eagle Cliff. Canned salmon tasted better and stayed fresher than fish preserved by the traditional methods of smoking or salting. The Hume brothers venture

was a success from the outset. Their first year of operation, four thousand cases of salmon were canned, with production quadrupling the next year. A canning dynasty was born. In 1881 there were thirty-five canneries along the Columbia, the four Hume brothers having established half of them.[8]

The advent of the Columbia River salmon canning industry coincided nicely with the introduction of the foremost piece of fishing gear used on the river. It was called a gillnet. First brought to the Columbia in 1853 from Maine's Kennebec River, the gillnet consisted of a rectangular piece of webbing weighted on the bottom by a lead-cored line and buoyed on top by a string of corks. It was laid across a stretch of river and allowed to drift in the current. As the salmon swam into the net their gills became entangled at which point the net was hauled aboard the fishing boat and the fish picked out. It was a most effective means of fishing. Several thousand gillnetters plied the Lower Columbia during the peak years of the salmon runs. The picturesque fleet became known as the "butterfly fleet" due to the peculiar wing-shape of the boat's sails.

Gillnetting has been a dangerous job from its inception, with scores of lives lost every season in the early decades. Because the first gillnets were made of flax and cotton threads they had to be fished in the darkness of night to prevent the fish from seeing the webbing. Navigating the frail sailing gillnet boats at night was always risky. One of the greatest disasters among the gillnet fleet occurred May 4, 1874 when a fierce squall hit unexpectedly. Boats were scattered and broken. Folklore measures the death toll in hundreds, but as stragglers kept turning up, the official count totaled twenty-six. Around 1905, powerboats replaced the butterfly fleet, making fishing somewhat safer and definitely more efficient.

By the mid-1870s, the north bank was dotted with canneries. In the late 1860s John West opened a cannery at Hungry Harbor; Ellis & Company at Point Ellice; George Hume at Knappton Cove in 1870; Around his cannery in 1873, Joe Megler established the hamlet of Brookfield, named for his wife's hometown in Massachusetts; and in 1878, a cannery started operations at Pillar Rock at the spot where William Clark first viewed the Columbia River estuary. The boom in cannery construction, however, was not limited to the river's north bank.

Irrespective of Astoria's notoriety as an early fur trading post, the salmon fisheries of the late nineteenth-century put it on the map. Astoria's first cannery began processing fish in Uppertown in 1873. Three years later, five canneries embraced its shores and by 1879, fourteen. Thanks to Astoria's deep anchorage, canned salmon could be loaded directly onto export ships, whereas most north-bank plants had to transport their product to deeper water to be shipped. During the season of 1877, eleven canneries churned out canned salmon, while over one thousand fishing boats plied the waters within eyeshot of the city. And the city boomed. Between 1874 and 1876, the population nearly doubled. Astoria was no longer a sleepy village.

Workers came in droves to man the canneries, the fishing boats, and various other growing industries. In 1876, the population reached 2,500, topping 6,000 in 1880, and doubling once again by 1900. Housing was in great demand. Many lived in crowed bunkhouses or boarding houses, but in short order ornate western Victorian houses augmented the log cabins and cramped quarters. Many of the canneries were located on the eastern end of town to shield the residences from the foul-smelling offal and byproducts carried on the prevailing westerly breezes. With the upshot in population, Astoria soon had two weekly newspapers and, for a time, held the title of Oregon's second largest city.

Astoria was not the only town to enjoy the returns of the salmon fishery. Chinook, downriver from old Chinookville, was home to hundreds of fish traps. The fact that a large portion of the returning salmon traversed the shallow shoals of Baker's Bay did not go unnoticed by observant locals. Largely unsuitable for gillnetting due to lack of sufficient depth, long rows of piling were driven in from which webbing was draped, herding the fish to a central collecting point, or trap. From there they were hoisted out of the water in a net and harvested. Countless salmon were gathered in these corral-like fish traps with remarkably little effort. The town of Chinook prospered. During the peak years of the salmon runs, Chinook was held locally to be the richest town, per capita, in the United States. It seemed every family had its own lucrative fish trap.

Ilwaco, another northshore community, thrived on salmon. Much of Ilwaco's salmon harvest came from fish traps positioned between Sand Island and Fort Canby. Ilwaco's history can be traced back to 1851 when Dr. Elijah White plotted a settlement he christened Pacific City. Blessed with a deep anchorage and a short, yet deep channel to the ocean, the town site seemed suffused with promise; but at the outbreak of the Civil War, the location became part of the military reservation surrounding Cape Disappointment. Once moved east, the new town became Unity in 1862 and eventually took the name Ilwaco in honor of Comcomly's son-in-law, Ilwaco Jim. And in 1880, B.A. Seaborg, a prosperous Finnish immigrant, built a salmon cannery that became the town's economic center. Seaborg, and a number of his fellow countrymen, had arrived on the coast as members of the first major wave of Finnish immigrants to make the Lower Columbia their home scarcely a decade before.

The salmon fishery brought fishermen from all points of the globe to Astoria. Ethnic clusters of Greeks, Portuguese, and assorted Scandinavians made residences there, but none more so than Finns. Born and raised in fishing and lumbering villages in the old country, the Finns fit the Lower Columbia perfectly. By the turn of the twentieth-century, half of Astoria's population could trace its roots to Finland, their number concentrated largely on the west end of town. For a time, Astoria had two Finnish-language newspapers, one of which could boast of having a circulation larger than all of Astoria's English-language papers combined.[9]

The Chinese were another group drawn to the Lower Columbia by the allure of the salmon fishery. Although the Chinese were not allowed to fish, virtually all canneries employed the skillful hands of Chinese workers to process fish. Their employment was first noted at the cannery at Eagle Cliff in 1872. In short order, Astoria developed a recognizable Chinatown along the waterfront near the canneries. By 1880, nearly one third of Clatsop County's population was Chinese.[10] The Chinese proved to be so adept at cleaning and trimming fish that, in 1905, when a machine was invented to do the task, it was given the bigoted title "Iron Chink." Its rotating knives could do the work of scores of men, greatly thinning the ranks of the cannery workers and consequently reducing the local population of East Asians.

Astoria's assortment of mostly vagrant fishermen quickly, and deservedly, earned the reputation of wild-men. Under the low glow of Astoria's coal oil street lamps, nighttime industries prospered. Astoria hosted, some say, more saloons per capita of population than any other town in Oregon, as well as one of the finest red-light districts to be found anywhere. In a well-cordoned section of town along the waterfront, a fisherman, cannery worker, or logger could find virtually anything to suit his fancy. The notorious string of brothels and bars lined the street named for the town's patriarch, Astor.

The lurid section of town surrounding Astor Street was given the dubious moniker "Swilltown." Though abhorred by

the upright citizens of Astoria, little was done to rid the city of the lowbrow element. It was simply too lucrative. Over one-third of the town's income in 1880 came from city-mandated liquor license fees. For all of its garish debauchery, "Swilltown" helped fund Astoria's streets, schools, and fire fighting equipment.[11] Furthermore, a large number of boarding houses and saloons were owned by outstanding citizens and leased for operation.

In 1880, an affable twenty-year-old Finn named August Erickson left his fishing boat for a life on Astoria's raucous waterfront. Sixteen years later he opened the town's most elegant saloon, The Louvre, in the heart of Astor Street. The three-storied establishment catered to all male tastes—fine spirits, billiards, an arcade, courtesans, and even a faddish roller-skating rink on the top floor. It was billed as a first-class drinkery with good order where "everybody's rights" are "strictly observed." Despite The Louvre's success, Erickson left Astoria, opening a bar—purportedly the West's largest—on Portland's Burnside Street. A mecca for the Northwest's thirsty loggers, mill workers, and sailors, Erickson's in Portland featured a legendary bar measuring 684 linear feet, taking up almost an entire city block.

Sailors worldwide knew of Astor Street. Its reputation came not only from the many indulgences offered there, but also from the ever-present danger of shanghaiing, or crimping as it was called. Alcohol, drugs, trickery, and even clubs were used to get unwary young men aboard ocean-bound ships where captains, in desperate need of able-bodied seamen, would pay "blood money" for delivery. Although aggrandized by folklore, crimping stood as a genuine concern to people traveling Astoria's waterfront at night.

One of Astoria's leading crimps was a diminutive Irish woman named Bridget Grant. This short-statured, gentle-faced boarding-house proprietor arrived in Astoria in 1876 after operating similar hostelries in Gloucester and San Francisco. Generally well respected by the community, this unassuming little woman's penchant for shanghaiing and extortion earned her the reputation "queen of the boarding-masters' fraternity." Together with her son Peter, a notorious Portland boardinghouse operator and crimp, Mrs. Grant collected her fair share of "blood money." Local tales relate that her farm on a seemingly remote tributary adjacent to Astoria was cleared by crimped labor, afraid to flee due to the unfamiliar surroundings.[12] Despite her dubious record, Mrs. Grant's three daughters were highly regarded schoolmarms and one of her sons the Astoria police chief. By the turn of the twentieth century, shanghaiing had all but disappeared from Astoria's waterfront.

In 1878, as crimping flourished, a road connecting Uppertown with downtown Astoria was completed, ending a rivalry born back in 1849 with the construction of the customs house. The customs house was relocated to lower Astoria in 1861, but in the meantime Uppertown had established its own schools, churches, cemeteries, and post office. With the road across Scow Bay connecting the two distinct boroughs, the assimilation process began and Uppertown's post office discontinued. Slowly the shallow bay was filled in. Nevertheless, Uppertown was not drawn into the official city limits until 1891.

❧

The year 1883 opened as one of the finest in Astoria's history. That year more salmon was canned than ever before at the highest price offered to date. The town's thirty canneries packed in excess of 620,000 cases of salmon, valued at over three million dollars. But the good times were not to last. On July 2, 1883, a fire started under a sawmill in the center of Astoria's waterfront. Supposedly some careless boys sparked the blaze in the tinderbox of dry shaving and sawdust under the mill. In any event, the structure was a sheet of flames before the city's fire companies had a chance to react. Businesses in Astoria were closed and all able hands put toward saving the heart of the city. In 1883 Astoria's fire protection consisted of two steam pumps, a hook-and-ladder company, and some antiquated hand pumps. They were of little use as the fire quickly spread from one establishment, across the wooden-planked streets, and on to the next. Furniture, kegs of whiskey, and any number of other goods were taken from flaming businesses and piled in the streets in an attempt to save them. The lower element of the city quickly consumed the unattended liquor, and the looting began. Shop owners and the local police force guarded the stock of remaining goods but to little avail.

As evening approached, the fire spread to the expansive Oregon Railroad & Navigation dock where some 10,000 cases of canned salmon were stored. As the canned juices came to a boil the tin cans ripped open with a small explosion, exposing the fatty salmon meat that smoldered in a smoky heap. The sound of bursting cans could be heard all night and through much of the following day.

Miraculously, the hospital was saved by bucket brigades spreading wetted bed covers over the roof. As darkness descended on the city, another sawmill and wharf were destroyed. That night the red glow of flaming rubble lit the streets. The fire crews continued to labor feverishly and were aided by a pump boat spraying water from the river. By the following morning, the fire had run its course and been contained but the thievery continued.

Left: From their introduction in the 1870s until their prohibition in the 1930s, fish traps were the mainstay of salmon fishing on Baker's Bay. North-bank communities like Ilwaco and Chinook depended almost exclusively on these salmon corrals to supply their canneries with fish.

The following day a vigilance committee was formed to recover the stolen merchandise. Headed by a leading shopkeeper, the committee issued a proclamation demanding all stolen items be returned to City Hall. It went unnoticed. So, with the blessing of local authorities, the citizen's committee took action. The following night, one of the leaders of the thieving horde, a barkeeper, was taken to the cemetery and given a choice: hanging or whipping. A rope was very deliberately thrown over a large limb in the nearby tree, and the barkeep quickly opted for the lashing. The following morning he gladly accepted passage on a Portland-bound steamer. The next evening the vigilance committee gave another thug the same option. Lashes once again. City Hall was soon inundated with returned merchandise.

The proprietors of one saloon, however, would not leave willingly. A group of special deputies and members of the vigilance committee descended upon the establishment. A pistol shot rang out and a gun battle ensued. One man inside the pub was wounded in the leg and the holdouts surrendered. Three men and a "woman of belligerent disposition" were taken into custody and made to leave town. A proclamation was issued to the remaining rabble-rousers reading: "Astoria, July 4th, 1883, To — —-, you are hereby notified to leave Astoria, within 24 hours, not to return. Signed Citizen's Committee." A number of pimps, crimps, and provocateurs left town, willingly, and others left without as much as an invitation to do so. With the dirty work behind them, the citizens of Astoria commenced celebrating the most somber Fourth of July in the city's history.

Rebuilding began at once. Gushing with proceeds from the incredible salmon pack, work proceeded quickly. Astoria's lone remaining sawmill worked day and night to churn out lumber for the ambitious project. The busy mill belonged to one of Astoria's leading industrialists, John C. Trullinger. This wildly successful entrepreneur had tried his hand at everything from panning gold to processing wheat to producing pig iron before settling in Astoria to oversee his newly constructed sawmill in the late 1870s. In the years that followed the fire of 1883, the timber industry became a crucial component of economic growth along the Columbia River estuary.

❧

Salmon was king in the big river, but timber reigned supreme in the adjacent tributary valleys. Lumber had been cut commercially along the Columbia since the Hudson's Bay Company started a small water-powered mill near Fort Vancouver in the late 1820s. Throughout the 1830s and 1840s, numerous sawmills sprouted on tributary streams con-

ducive to water-wheel operations. Astoria's first sawmill dates back to 1851. Besides cutting for local markets, sawmills found eager buyers in California, especially San Francisco following the outbreak of gold fever. The pattern was set.

To supply sawmills on the Lower Columbia loggers took to the woods with ax in hand. The maritime rain forests grew trees with diameters and heights these woodsmen had never before encountered. In coastal lowlands, cedar and spruce grew to diameters sometimes in excess of twenty feet. But the predominant and most sought-after species was "Oregon pine", named for David Douglas, the Scot botanist who first classified it: Douglas fir. These towering fir giants could reach heights of over three hundred feet from roots to crown, with diameters averaging six feet. With unparalleled grit and determination, loggers set to work toppling these giants. Because water was the easiest means of transporting logs, early loggers simply felled trees into the stream, limbed them, cut them to length, and towed them in groups, or rafts, to the nearest mill which was never far. Some of the notable early hotbeds of logging were along the John Day, Walluski, and Youngs rivers in Oregon, and the Chinook, Deep, and Grays rivers on the Washington side.

As the timberline receded from the riverbank, loggers began to devise new methods for getting logs into the water. Hand-loggers used crank-jacks and peaveys to manhandle the mammoth logs, but their range was limited. More resourceful loggers used hulking steers called bulls to skid the logs to tributary streams. A path was first cleared and at suitable intervals small logs were placed in the roadbed perpendicular to the trail, creating what loggers termed a skidroad. Once such a trail was completed, multiple yokes of oxen were chained to incredible strings of logs and at the teamster, or bullwhacker's, command they commenced to tug the gargantuan sticks over the skidroads free from miring in the mud or hanging up on rocks. In front of the team, a logger known as a "grease monkey" ran along dabbing grease or tallow on the skids to reduce friction. When everything was clicking it worked beautifully, but even the bull teams had their limits.

In the 1880s, steam power, in the form of the steam donkey, was introduced to the woods of the Lower Columbia. Cheaper to operate and more efficient by far, steam donkeys could drag logs distances that bull-team loggers could only dream of. By the outbreak of World War I, high-lead logging had become the new standard. In a tall spar, well guyed to surrounding stumps, huge pulleys or blocks were hung and steel cables ran out from the donkey, through the blocks, to the cut timber. Short noose-like chokers attached to one of these cables were fastened to the logs, the donkey engineer

Right: Standing atop their spring boards to avoid the tree's butt-swell, two timber fallers pose by a freshly chopped "undercut" which will direct the tree's fall.

A view down Astoria's Commercial Street in the 1890s illustrates the city's hallmark planked streets and ornate wooden architecture.

was given a signal, and the logs came in a-snorting suspended over obstacles of all sorts. At the spar, the logs were loaded onto railroad cars and brought out of the hills where they were dumped into streams and mill ponds. One of the earliest operations to utilize both steam donkeys and a railroad belonged to Astoria's John C. Trullinger.

In 1885, Trullinger expanded his business beyond sawmills and logging to open Astoria's first electric-light generating plant, run off waste from his sawmill. An 1890 upgrade in the facility, at which time a 2,000-lamp incandescent generator was added, allowed citizens of the city to light their houses with Thomas Edison's newly perfected glowing filament.[13] Economically stable, Trullinger turned to politics. A staunch Republican, he served a term as an Oregon state legislator, and reigned as mayor-elect of Astoria from 1886 to

1888 when talk of mass-transit first began to swirl.

Astoria took an essential step to becoming a veritable city when, on a summer day in 1888, passenger service was inaugurated on the newly completed trolley line. Although it took a number of tries, in its fourth incarnation the Astoria Street Railway Company succeeded. Horses pulled the handsome little four-wheeled trolley coaches. The clop of horse hooves could be heard throughout the ever-expanding system of three-foot gauge track laid on the city's wooden-planked streets. With the stringing of wires and the raising of poles, the tracks, electrified in the spring of 1892, sent the horses, proverbially, out to pasture.

Throughout the late 1880s and 1890s, fishing continued to be a stable source of revenue for Astoria. The peak of the Columbia River salmon fishery came in 1895 when 635,000 cases of salmon were put up.[14] In the 1880s, the fishermen organized, forming the Columbia River Fishermen's

Protective Union. Collectively, it was believed, a better price for fish could be bargained. In addition, so-called "snag unions" were created to clear gillnet drifts of snags, sinkers, and debris. In the mid-1890s, the canneries followed suit, establishing the Columbia River Packers' Association, which as intended, helped the associated canneries better sell their products and stabilize market conditions. Also, much to the fishermen's chagrin, it gave the canneries the ability to set the price for salmon.

In reaction to the formation of the omnipotent Columbia River Packers' Association, the commercial fishermen of the lower river went on strike during the summer salmon run of 1896. The enraged fishermen demanded five cents per pound for their catch, but the united canneries were unwilling to pay. The gillnetters adopted the motto: "Five Cents or No Fish!" As the strike dragged on, tensions grew. By the tenth week, the uneasiness in Astoria crested and the mayor was forced to call upon the Oregon State Militia to ensure peace. On June 16, 1896, the steamer Harvest Queen rounded Tongue Point from Portland with nearly five hundred soldiers of the First Regiment onboard. The assemblage set up camp near the courthouse, their daily drills becoming a popular spectacle for Astoria's citizenry. Armed troops were posted at several canneries, and the steamer Dwyer armed with a gatling gun was chartered for river patrol.

Meanwhile, on Baker's Bay, many of the fish traps continued to operate throughout the strike. A great deal of animosity was aroused, resulting in the destruction of a number of fish traps at the hands of angry gillnetters. In response, Washington's governor called upon his state's militia to protect the property of the trap fishermen. It should be noted that the strife between the gillnetters and trap fishermen would not be fully resolved until the 1930s when the traps were prohibited by law.

Heavily dependent on revenue from fishing, most businesses in Astoria had temporarily closed their doors by early June 1896. Pressured by the business sector and the presence of the state militia, the Fishermen's Union held a "long and earnest" meeting on June 20. In a close vote, with only a fifty-seven percent majority, the fishermen agreed to settle on the compromise price of four and one-half cents per pound. "There was a general feeling of relief throughout the city last night," declared The Daily Morning Astorian, after word circulated that the "great strike" had ended. Reluctantly, the fishermen returned to the water and businesses resumed daily affairs. After the conclusion of the longest fishing strike in Columbia River history, the militia left Astoria, the last soldier departing the morning of June 24.

By the time of the great strike it was obvious that the salmon runs were not unlimited. Unregulated fishing pressure had taken its toll. The salmon pack had plummeted from 630,000 cases in 1883 to 400,000 in 1887.[15] So in 1887, Washington's Territorial Governor made two visits to the

A fine catch of Columbia River salmon, probably from a seining operation.

Columbia River demanding that local authorities bring illegal fishing to a stop, and attempting to convince fishing industry officials that some balance must be struck. "The salmon fisheries of the Columbia and other Washington Territory rivers will yield from two to three million dollars per annum according to the season for an indefinite time," he cautioned the Legislature, "if prudently and economically managed." He predicted at the current rate of harvest, "the industry will be destroyed within the next five years."[16]

Progressive local citizens began to talk about creating a fish hatchery. Chinook residents knew of a man with nearly a decade of experience in salmon propagation. His name was Alfred E. Houchen. After jumping a British sloop-of-war in Victoria, B.C. shortly after the American Civil War, Houchen worked his way south as riverboatman, logger, lumberman, and finally as a gillnetter and cannery operator. He then settled down to a quieter life on a tideland ranch on Bear River, north of Chinook, where he built his own private salmon hatchery. For his knowledge of salmon he was appointed Washington State deputy fish commissioner in the early 1890s. Under Houchen's watchful eye, the Chinook Salmon Hatchery was built on the Chinook River in 1895. It was the first of its kind in the state of Washington.[17]

Soured by the strike of 1896 and declining salmon runs, a number of Astoria's fishermen took action. In the fall of that year, two hundred gillnetters, many of them Finns, banded together to form the Union Fishermen's Cooperative Packing Company. Eager craftsmen had a cannery built and operating by the time the salmon began to return to the river the following spring. High quality and peerless standards kept the label competitive in an ever-restricting market. The Finnish sector of town, dubbed "Uniontown," under today's Astoria-Megler bridge, takes its name from the cooperative that was located there. Expanding into canning deep-sea fish like tuna, the plant continued operation under the ownership of Barbey Packing Corporation into the second half of the twentieth-century.

Even with the unpredictability of the salmon runs, catches remained awe-inspiring even after the dawn of the new century. The greatest one-day haul ever recorded belongs to Astoria gillnetter Peter Dorcich. In July 1904, Dorcich single-handedly harvested 4,495 pounds of Chinook salmon in two consecutive drifts. In his first drift he fished past Peacock Spit, hauling in 101 salmon, totaling 2,595 pounds, before catching the flood tide and sailing back up the river. He then proceeded to lay his net a second time, catching another ton of fish. His profit from that noteworthy day went unrecorded, but the cannery to which he was selling paid five cents per pound, with deductions for oversized fish. Dorcich probably netted in excess of $220.[18] Another Astoria gillnetter, Ben Johnson, probably holds the single-season fishing record. During the season of 1913, he caught 46,800 pounds of salmon.

❧

The entire region boomed with the completion of the transcontinental railroad to the Pacific Northwest in 1883. Overnight, wooden villages became cities of brick and stone. Tens of thousands of newcomers arrived by rail, but a growing portion arrived aboard ship. In response, the United States government purchased the old Hume cannery at Knappton Cove and renovated the isolated building into a quarantine station. New York Harbor's Ellis Island opened only seven years before the Quarantine Station at Knappton. Ships entering the Columbia were inspected at Astoria and sent to Knappton Cove if quarantine or fumigation was required. The first year of operation the station served 133 ships. Burning pots of sulfur sanitized the ship, while needy patients were treated in the newly constructed

medical facility. The "Columbia River's Ellis Island," as it was sometimes called, operated until 1928 when the quarantine office was relocated to Portland, the facility permanently closing in 1938.

Astoria, bound by water on three sides, collectively wanted a share of the prosperity enjoyed by other cities with railroads. Since the 1850s, the progressive residents of Astoria had desired a rail connection with the outside world. A number of fly-by-night railroads were incorporated during the 1860s and 1870s, but little work was completed. When Henry Villard, Oregon's greatest railroad builder, completed the Northern Pacific Railroad line to Portland in 1883 the Astoria connection seemed forthcoming. Villard, however, built the railroad down the Columbia's south bank only to Goble, fifty-eight miles east of Astoria. He did not see a line to the coast as essential because it was cheaper to ship goods down river from Portland—coincidently he owned controlling interest in a line of steamships—than to construct the remaining mileage to the river's mouth. Disappointment reigned over Astoria.

Undeterred, prosperous Astorians pooled their capital, determined to build a line up Youngs River, and along the Nehalem River to Portland. This project too went to ruin. Again in the early 1890s, a company was incorporated to build this southern route. Numerous miles were graded and a tunnel under Saddle Mountain begun before the financing dried up. In the meantime, a successful railroad had been completed in 1890 between Young's Bay and Seaside. Incorporated as the Astoria & South Coast Railway, the fifteen-mile line operated predominantly during the summer months carrying passengers to coastal resort towns. The success of the Seaside line offered little in the way of consolation to the citizens of Astoria.

Astoria's belated railroad salvation came by way of Andrew B. Hammond, a wealthy financier with track-laying experience. Hammond began work on the Astoria & Columbia River Railroad to connect with the Northern Pacific at Goble in 1896 with a lucrative subsidy contract that included several thousand acres of choice land in the greater Astoria area. The last spike was driven near Clatskanie on April 3, 1898. Astorians were elated. The line was then connected to the Astoria & South Coast system but the new road, despite showing earnings, did not bring Astorians the substantial commercial gains they had hoped for. Hammond began discussing the possibilities of southern extensions but before the plans could go ahead he sold the line to James J. Hill in 1907.

The same railroad craze that consumed Astoria was no less felt on the river's north bank. In 1890, a boomtown on Grays Bay threatened, at least on paper, to depose Astoria as the major seaport city at the river's mouth. Touted as westernmost terminus of James J. Hill's Northern Pacific Railroad, the city promised to be the San Francisco of the

FIRST TRAIN TO PORTLAND
A&CRR MAY 16 1898

The morning of May 16, 1898 dawned damp and misty as a crowd of Astorians gathered to see the Astoria & Columbia River Railroad's locomotive No. 1361 depart with the first eleven passenger coaches making the run to Portland. Piles of lumber clutter the planked platform—remains from the construction of the new depot.

Columbia. It was called Frankfort. The brainchild of James F. Bourn and Frank Scott, Frankfort had a short and rocky boom. The Frankfort Land Company, which owned some 8,000 lots, all reasonably priced, of course, financed a short-lived newspaper, The Frankfort Chronicle, first published in May 1892.[19] But, sadly for Frankfort, a national economic panic arrived in the mid-1890s and the Northern Pacific never laid tracks down the river's north bank. To this day, accessible only by water, Frankfort lingered as a minuscule colony of fishermen and misanthropes for over fifty years after its inception.

ॐ

While settlers and schemers dreamed of transcontinental railroads, work was getting underway to improve shipping across the Columbia Bar. Fighting stubborn winds and the roaring bar, sailing vessels had to wait off the coast, sometimes for weeks, before conditions permitted a crossing. In the spring of 1885, work began on an immense jetty to remedy, at least in part, this unruly bar. A short railroad was built along the proposed jetty's course and huge boulders cast off either side. It took ten years and multiple appropriations to complete the five-mile-long south jetty which worked beautifully. It not only stabilized the, bar but flushed the middle sands out to sea and deepened the channel. More work was done and by 1914 the south jetty neared seven miles in length.

Between 1914 and 1916, a north jetty took shape, built in a similar fashion, this one two miles long. Some of the rocks dumped from the rail cars weighed in excess of fifty tons. Now, funneled by a jetty on each extreme, the river split Peacock Spit, greatly improving shipping safety. Yet, despite

the advances, the river never reached the fifty-foot depth predicted by engineers, making constant dredging a necessity.

As the jetties took shape at the river's mouth, Astoria began to look back at one hundred years of continual settlement. Astoria, as a community, has long had a sense of history. In 1871, the interested citizenry organized the Pioneer and Historical Society. There was no doubt then that a grand celebration would be planned for the centennial of 1911. The centennial would involve all of the Northwest, not just Astoria proper. Preparations began in 1910 with consultants experienced in state and national celebrations being called in to share ideas and the significance of the occasion did not go unnoticed. A spokesperson for the Portland Chamber of Commerce noted "Centennial success means a greater Astoria." Work began on Centennial Park above Youngs Bay where an exact replica of Fort Astoria was constructed, surrounded by grandstands and bleachers.

The year-long celebration began April 12, 1911, exactly a century after the first Astorian set foot on Point George.

Speeches and ceremonies marked the event. The Scandinavian community hosted a full week of pageantry, including an extravagant parade. Members of the Nez Perce and Yakima tribes joined the local Chinooks and Clatsops in regaling the audience with traditional dance ceremonies. Ten thousand visitors thronged Centennial Park to witness the commemoration. It was building up to be Astoria's finest hour.

In August 1911, the official celebration opened with the sounding of a gong in Centennial Park, activated by an electric button pressed by President Taft himself back in Washington D.C. Dignitaries, including Oregon's Governor Oswald West and John Barrett, a presidential aide, spoke before the overflowing grandstands. Barrett read a message prepared by the president offering "hearty congratulations on the wonderful prosperity that has marked the development of that region." A large parade, declared by an Astoria paper to be the "best ever seen in the West," proceeded through the crowded downtown streets. After dark, an impressive array of

During World War I, construction trains dumped countless boulders, some weighing as much as fifty tons, onto the course that eventually became the North Jetty. The rocks were quarried in pits along the river and brought to the railhead by barge where they were transferred to railcars for final delivery.

fireworks lit the night sky, as well as the "grand illumination" of the city featuring some 12,000 lights.

But, in true Astoria tradition, not all went as planned. The world's tallest flagpole, a Douglas fir nearly two hundred-twenty feet tall, was harvested near Knappa and brought to Astoria. The Astoria Daily Budget declared it the "pride of the city." Everything went smoothly as the city crews began to raise the lengthy leviathan. Just as the pole reached its vertical position an improperly fastened guy wire snapped sending the fir crashing to the ground. In an instant the world's tallest flagpole became seven much, much shorter ones. Undeterred, organizers ordered another lanky fir pole from the forest behind Knappa, this one some two hundred-thirty feet in length. With a little more care the new pole went up without a hitch and was later sent to the Panama-Pacific Exposition in San Francisco as a gift from Oregon's oldest city.[20]

Another unfortunate folly was the exhibition of flight, one of the first of its kind in Clatsop County. Aviator Hugh Robinson was brought in to demonstrate his Curtis hydroplane. In front of a packed audience at Uniontown, Robinson took off on the first of three days of flights. Flying above the Columbia at roughly fifty miles per hour for half an hour, Robinson circled ships and did an assortment of tricks. The crowd was mesmerized. The second day of the flights proved to be anticlimactic. While attempting to take off, the plane struck the wake of a passing boat, breaking the propeller and sending the craft tumbling. Robinson escaped uninjured, but the ebb tide pulled his plane downriver and under the water's surface. It was quickly raised but, upon examination, was found to be damaged too badly for further flights.[21]

ASTORIA'S HEART IN RUI[N]

The Portland Telegram

THE WEATHER
Tonight snow, turning to rain; not so cold; Saturday rain; winds becoming southeasterly.

WARMER

6th Year.

PORTLAND, OREGON, FRIDAY EVENING, DECEMBER 8, 1922

PRICE ON TRAINS, BOATS, NEWS STANDS AND IN O[UT] SIDE CITIES, 5 CENTS; ON STREETS, 2 CEN[TS]

The best features... news that's true, s[o] well told and a bi[g] of features make Telegram Portland's newspaper for the f[...]

Views of Astoria, Swept by Greatest Conflagration in History of Pacific Northwest

HOEFLER'S CENTENNIAL CHOCOLATES

ASTORIA ORE © PRENTISS

GIFFORD & PRENTISS
PORTLAND, OREGON

ABOVE AT LEFT: Astoria—Weinhard hotel, chief hostelry, destroyed. Below: H. R. Hoefler's Centennial Chocolate plant, also lost. Birdseye view of Astoria with main part of burned district under reader's eye. Below: Another view of Astoria's burned district. (Pictures copyright by A. M. Prentiss.) Dotted line gives outline of burned area.

[STR]UCTURES AND [O]FFICES IN [A] FIERY PILE

Every Big Retail Structure Destroyed or Damaged Beyond Repair in Business Section of City.

[WEINHARD] HOTEL IS BURNED

[Fla]mes Make Clean Sweep of [C]ommercial Area; Docks, [P]ost Office and Court [H]ouse Alone Saved.

ASTORIA, Ore., Dec. 8.—[The] fire had reached Seventeenth street at 11:15 [o']clock, destroying the Astoria Business college, the [...]el Transfer block and [cen]tral fire station.

[B]uildings adjoining the [city] hall are burning.

[C]hief of Police Carlson [had] received a report that [an] unidentified citizen had [kill]ed himself during the [exc]itement.

ASTORIA, Ore., Dec. 8.— [(Spe]cial.)—A loss that will [run] into a score of million [dolla]rs—how much nobody [can] say—faces Astoria citizens today with the destruction of the business heart of [the c]ity—but Astoria is not [dism]ayed. It is calmly listing [its l]osses, and already thinking of how it will rebuild.

[A]t a check at 11 o'clock, [as n]ear exactly as could be [told u]nder the circumstances, [was t]he following buildings [raze]d by the mad sweep of [the] flames:

[We]inhard hotel.
[Bee]hive department store.
[Ho]efler confectionery.
[J.] C. Penny store.
[Asto]ria Budget, newspaper.
[Asto]ria theater.
[Odd] Fellows' hall.
[We]stern Union Telegraph [offic]es.
[I]rwyn hotel.
[Sta]ples Motor company.
[Elk]s' club.
[Od]d Men's hall.
[Fir]st National bank.
[Asto]ria Savings bank.
[Asto]ria National bank.
[Colu]mbia Trust & Savings [Ban]k.
[Ban]k of Commerce.
[Ha]llerud's dry goods stores.
[Asto]ria drug store.
[Cen]tral drug store.
[Mor]ton drug store.
[Ol]d drug store.
[Owe]n & Lewis, wholesale [groc]ery.
[John]son-Ehrman, wholesale [groc]ery.
[Bla]ck Mouse theater.
[Libe]rty theater.
[St]ar theater.
[Y. M.] C. A. building.
[Asto]ria Business college.
[Mor]ning Astorian.
[City] laundry.
[C]ity Opera house.
[This c]ity building, largest in [city, f]our stories high and cover[ing a] quarter block.
[...]l garage, covering half a [cit]y ground.
[...] A. badly damaged.
[Bu]ildings apparently doomed at [go t]o] press included:
[Cath]olic church.
[Asto]ria fire station.
[City] Business college.

SEX MAN IS FREED

CITY'S HISTORY LINKED WITH DEVELOPMENT AND GROWTH OF NORTHWEST

ASTORIA, the oldest town in Oregon, was founded April 12, 1811, by John Jacob Astor, American merchant, who opened the first American fur trading post in the Pacific Northwest. Prosperity loomed for the little city, but the War of 1812 stopped his enterprise.

The English took possession of the post in 1813, renamed it Fort St. George, and held it until 1818, though until 1846 the Northwest company, an English company of fur traders, continued to occupy it.

The natural antipathy between natives of the British empire and the United States is believed to have made imposible the successful establishment of Astoria as a fur trading post operated by Americans, for the inbred national prejudice of the Britisher for anything American was too powerful to go unrealized.

HELD BY BRITISH.

The British government transmitted orders to the agent of the Northwest company to deliver the post to the United States company to deliver the post operated by Americans.

The English took possession of the post operated by Americans.

In 1824 a bill for "the occupation of the Columbia river" appeared in the house. In 1825 the bill came up again. Both times it was laid on the table, and, in 1829, dropped. It was not until settlers began filling the post that the matter, except for

time under the control of the Northwest company.

Conditions continued on practically the same basis until 1821, when a resolution was introduced in congress instructing the committee on military affairs to "inquire into the expediency of making an appropriation to enable the president to take and retain possession of the territories of the United States on the northwest coast of America."

RIVER GATEWAY PRIZED.

The advisability of effecting the possession of the mouth of the Columbia river, pointed out to be a British loop hole for ultimate possession of all United States territory beyond the Rocky mountains, was seen by many statesmen. The resolution was adopted, but no action was taken.

BUT ONE DEAD, CHECK SHOWS

Early Rumors of Many Fatalities Seem Unfounded When Check Made.

ASTORIA, Ore., Dec. 8.—(Special)—Rumors of many fatalities in today's disastrous fire were current here early this morning, but when a check had been made at 11 o'clock, it appeared that Morris Staples was the only victim.

He died apparently from exhaustion while pushing automobiles from the Staples Motor company's garage when the fire had reached that point.

He also was president of the Astoria Bank of Commerce.

It was erroneously reported that W. H. Fellman was dead also, but he later appeared, sound and well.

DEATH CAR NOT UNDER CONTROL, IS VERDICT

HILLSBORO, Ore., Dec. 8.—(Spe-

NORTHWEST IS READY TO AID

Portland Telegram Among First to Offer Succor to Astoria Citizens.

All Oregon—and the Northwest, too, for that matter—was touched this morning by Astoria's plight, and offers of aid began to pour in on the city at the mouth of the Columbia. Among the first to offer assistance was The Portland Telegram.

Mayor J. Brenner was called by long distance phone by O. C. Leiter, managing editor of The Portland Telegram and told that this publication would dispatch a special train, if necessary, with any food supplies, tents, cots or other articles needed.

Mayor Brenner planned to call citizens into conference and determine if any outside help would be asked for.

STORES ALL GONE.

"All our stores are wiped out." said the mayor, and it is probable that we will have to ask that food supplies be rushed into Astoria from outside points.

"We are in such turmoil that it is difficult at this time to form any idea of our needs.

"Our town is ruined; but it is too early to say that the business houses will be rebuilt or will not be rebuilt.

"We will make a complete survey as soon as we have checked the fire—that is engaging all our attention at this hour (9:30 a. m.) and we still have an enormous task before us in fighting the flames.

"Aid will be accepted gladly, if we find we need it."

Relief—food supplies, medical service or whatever else is most needed in Astoria—will be rushed from Portland by special train as soon as it has been ascertained that it is most needed.

Various agencies already have offered their services for this purpose.

WILL MAKE SURVEY.

RAILROADS TO HELP.

W. D. Skinner, general traffic manager of the Seattle, Portland & Spokane, has promised the full cooperation of the railway to get relief and supplies transported, and W. D. B. Dodson, secretary manager of the Chamber of Commerce, has called a conference of the "jobbers of Portland to meet at the chamber to...

TELEPHONE GIRLS STICK AT INSTRUMENTS UNTIL FLAMES REACH BUILDING

AS USUAL, the heroines of the Astoria fire were the telephone operators, who remained at their switchboards in the telephone building until they were driven out by flames that surrounded the structure.

A Portland Telegram staff member was talking from Portland to Miss J. Hitchcock, chief operator, at 6 o'clock this morning. Miss Hitchcock was describing the fire as it appeared from her point of vantage, when suddenly she broke in with the words:

"Sorry, but we're ordered out; goodbye."

Fannie Carlson, Josephine Bobert, Mabel Wiggins, Pearl Hakala, Mrs. Pearl Gore, Marie Townsend, Rosella Wellington, Irma Stafford, Peggy Lokan, Hilda Lake, Ellen Anderson, Rose Aviana and Henrietta Ysted.

MANY WITNESSES YET TO BE HEARD IN CASE

OXFORD, Miss., Dec. 8.—With more than a score of witnesses, including Theodore G. Bilbo, former

---

FIRE [...] 35 [...] LO[SS]

Flames Piling and B[...] Blazin[g]

$15,00[0]

Dynamite Ravage[s] When [...] paratu[s]

The Pac[ific] pany's [...] went out [at] 10:25 th[is] Hickman, superinter[...] land offic[e...] would ind[...] hall at A[...] reached b[y] operators [...] temporary [...] building, [...]

Hickm[an...] building w[...] the adjoin[ing...] dynamited [...] check the [...]

ASTORI[A...] (Special.)—[...] its busine[ss...] by fire an[d...] lower re[...] ashes, one [of...] zens dead [...] less serio[us...] toria, the [...] state of [...] today was [...] on the ba[ck...] reaches of [...] Norris S[...] the Ban[k...] dropped de[...] the flames [...] zens. [...]

Probably [...] two blocks [...] of the city [...] yond repai[r...] is a fringe [...] buildings, [...] have to be [...]

LOSS [...]
W. A. Tyl[er...] leading ba[...] the loss at [...] 000 and [...] only twent[y...] fire swept. [...] tional prop[erty...] area will [...] this figure [...]

The blaze [...] ace cafe on [...]

(Conclude[d...]

TEL[...] EXT[...] ASTO[...]

The disas[ter...] was known [...] stir from a [...] son of an o[...] 7:30 o'clock [...] only reach [...] full accoun[t...] up to that ti[me...] stroyed was [...] the import[ant...] Portland on [...] published m[...] ing out the [...]

Formerly Astoria's grandest hostelry, the Weinhard-Astoria Hotel was leveled by the great fire.

Astoria continued to grow through World War I, becoming home to a lucrative wartime shipbuilding contract. But after the war came another setback, by far the most devastating in city history. During the unusually dry night of Friday, December 7, 1922, fire once again broke out in the heart of the riverside city. Fire crews rushed to tame the flames, but as water mains under the city's wooden streets erupted, pressure plummeted. The city was helpless. People from Ilwaco and Chinook gathered at Point Ellice to watch the distant inferno. By sunrise the next morning, with a light dusting of snow on the city, nearly thirty city blocks lay in ruin including the plush Weinhard-Astoria Hotel. Compounding the tragedy was the fact that less than fifty percent of the ravaged real estate was covered by insurance due to the high rates available in the combustible old wooden city.[22] The Oregon National Guard quickly mobilized, heading off any looting that might occur. When rebuilding started, city planners, having learned a lesson from Astoria's other great fire of 1883, insisted on replacing wooden-planked streets with pavement, filling around the piling with rubble and fill. In addition, the fire of 1922 effectively ended Astoria's trolley system, favoring busses instead.

Building a monument on Coxcomb Hill, the large rise on Astoria's southern boarder, had long been discussed. It was not until the aftermath of the fire of 1922 that definite action began taking place. With money provided by John Jacob Astor's descendants and the Northern Pacific Railroad, New York architect Electus D. Litchfield was hired to design and construct a column atop the hill. Sculptor Attilio Pusterla was employed to carve images depicting local history in the sgraffito style whereby an outside layer of mortar was chipped away to expose a darker inside layer. Work began on April Fools Day 1926 and was completed in July.

From atop the Astoria Column one could look down through the salt-washed air upon the hills of beautiful Western Victorian homes and shapely church steeples gracing the city. With sawmills and canneries humming below, imagining Astoria's high times would not be difficult. Beyond the industrial waterfront stretched the great river of the West, and on its north bank, Washington. In the spring, salmon still swim past Astoria, albeit in diminished numbers, passing Pillar Rock, the site at which an exuberant William Clark first sighted the expansive Columbia River Estuary.

Left: The destruction of Astoria's downtown made news throughout the Northwest.

Below: *Fort Canby, located along the southwestern extreme of Baker's Bay, was built by Union forces during the Civil War. Encompass Cape Disappointment, the fort is named in honor of Major-General Edwards R.S. Canby, a West Point graduate originally from Kentucky, who perished in the Modoc War (1872-73) only two years after transferring to Oregon. In 1878, Fort Canby became a lifesaving station due to its proximity to the "Graveyard of the Pacific."*

Left: *Mighty boulders en route to be dumped into the Pacific Ocean to form a jetty at the river's mouth.*

Right: *The Port Docks of Astoria catered to many vessels, including the local ship* Chillicothe.

Previous spread: *In a scene reminiscent of Alfred Hitchcock, seagulls swarm the four-masted* Star of Shetland, *one of the many ships to take on cargo on the Columbia River.*

The British bark Galena *went ashore on Clatsop Beach on the dark, blustery night of November 13, 1906 inbound from Chile. The 292-foot vessel had been lying off the Columbia Bar waiting for a pilot when heavy seas carried her onto the beach.*

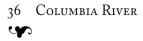

The lower Columbia experiences up to 10-foot tides and between 80 to 130 inches of rain per year. From November until early summer, before the creation of hard surface roads, rain-soaked mud roads created almost impassible quagmires. Fortunately many sloughs and river and creek estuaries created hundreds of miles of tidal waters that at high tide were easily navigated by large, flat-bottomed, boats.

It is not unknown for the Columbia River to freeze, from one bank to the other.

The Oregon Coast was revered, and even feared, by sailors worldwide for its unpredictable nature.

Top: With much of her crew asleep, the American bark Harvest Home *ran aground near Long Beach in the dense fog of the pre-dawn hours on January 18, 1882. A defective chronometer was faulted for the foundering, but all hands walked ashore safely, although the vessel was lost.*

Bottom: Four spectators pose on the wrecked hull of the German brig Potrimpos, *grounded due to strong winds and heavy seas December 19, 1896 north of Long Beach, Washington.*

Top: Life savers, or surfmen, from the Klipsan Beach Life Saving Station rush to rescue the crew of the floundering ship Alice. *The life saving station, placed on the National Register of Historic Sites in 1979, stood watch over Washington's Long Beach Peninsula from 1889 until after World War II. All hands aboard the* Alice *reached shore safely.*

Bottom: The French ship Alice *went ashore on the Long Beach Peninsula in the early morning hours of January 15, 1909. Her 3,000-ton cargo of cement solidified after being exposed to water, making salvage efforts impossible.*

Fr~Brk·ALICE·WKd· Jan-15-09 · Ocean Park WA

"Solano, Stranded near Ocean Park, Wash.

Left: Hopelessly stranded, the weather-beaten sails of the British ship Peter Iredale *rest tattered along Clatsop Beach, wrecked October 25, 1906.*

Top: Impenetrable fog sometimes shrouds the shipping lanes of the Columbia, and from time to time, has been disadvantageous to shippers. These two freighters, the Welsh Prince *and the* Iowan, *collided off the Washington fishing village of Altoona, May 28, 1922.*

Bottom: A surf-beaten hull is all that remains of the once-proud four-masted schooner Solano *stranded February 5, 1907 near Ocean Park, Washington, in this undated photo.*

Bottom: One of the most noted ship wrecks along the Oregon coast is the 287-foot British vessel Peter Iredale, *which went ashore in the early morning hours of October 25, 1906. Still visible to this day, her hull is a major tourist attraction at Fort Stevens State Park.*

Top: A steam-powered tug assists a sailing vessel across the south approach to the Columbia Bar.

Right: During wartime, Astoria geared up for the production of naval vessels.

Top: *Six sailing vessels lay at anchor in front of Astoria. Hundreds of windjammers called on the Columbia every year, many bound for the growing metropolis of Portland.*

Bottom: *Astoria has had a long tradition of being home to some of the finest boat and ship builders along the West Coast. Here, under construction are lifeboats in the Wickstrom and Nyman boat shop.*

Standing akimbo by his prized halibut, the elated fisherman gives perspective on just how big a 228-pound fish truly is.

Top: Five gillnet boats enjoy a free ride behind a steamer as one grateful fisherman salutes the camera with his hat.

Bottom: Apron-clad cannery workers labor to clean and process a bountiful catch of chinook salmon.

Previous Spread: In order to keep their gillnets from snagging on debris at the river's bottom, gillnetters created "snag unions" to work collectively at keeping their drifts clear.

Top: Hauling the seine net on an exposed spit on the Lower Columbia River.

Bottom: Derbyville, located between Chinook and Megler, was a popular spot for sport fishermen, and, as the name asserts, was home to a number of salmon fishing derbies. These sport fishermen, utilizing a cannery-owned gillnet boat, bring a nice chinook salmon aboard off Derbyville.

Top: Waist deep in the frigid waters of the Columbia, horse seiners prepare to collect their haul.

Bottom left: With muscles straining, this well-dressed fisherman poses for a photo with a nice king, or chinook, salmon, the largest species of salmon to enter the Columbia.

Bottom right: Women at a Columbia River Packers' Association cannery work on an assembly line of tin cans. The first major segment of the population to work in the canneries was the Chinese, but by the mid-twentieth century much of the work force was composed of women.

Bottom: Countless fathoms of gillnets are draped over the net racks at the Union Fishermen's Co-operative Packing Company in west Astoria, named Uniontown after the cannery's title. Opened for the spring fishery of 1897, this venerable old packing plant stood as one of Astoria's most notable waterfront landmarks until the second half of the twentieth century.

Top: As salmon runs and financial returns diminished, canneries in Astoria turned to processing ocean fish, like tuna shown here.

Top: When gillnetters were not fishing they could always find something to do. Here busy fishermen tend to their gillnets draped over net racks, once a common sight along Astoria's waterfront.

Bottom: Nearly swamped, a sturgeon-laden gillnet boat lies moored to the dock at Nahcotta, Washington, on the northeast side of the Long Beach Peninsula. The commercial harvest of sturgeon has always been limited on both the Columbia River and Willapa Bay due to the prehistoric fish's slow regeneration cycle.

Four massive logs wait to be rolled onto railroad cars near Svenson, Oregon, prior to World War I.

During the Depression, small logging firms, known as gypos, began harvesting timber along the Lower Columbia. Using log trucks and bulldozers as an alternative to high-cost railroad operations, gypos soon became prevalent.

Previous page: With the advent of high-lead logging methods, a new occupation was born: high climbing, also known as high rigging. Only the bravest of loggers took to the profession of cutting the tops out of towering trees and hanging heavy blocks in the spar. Sometimes, however, the high climbers' bravery bordered on insanity.

The ever-churning currents of the Pacific Ocean deposit all sorts of secrets along this coastline. Here a giant log has been salvaged from the beach sand on the Long Beach Peninsula.

Keeping the steam up in a steam donkey required a lot of chord wood, but firewood was much cheaper and more accessible than hay for the bull teams that fueled the timber industry before steam donkeys.

Next spread: Relaxing among sword ferns and slash, five loggers in Washington's Grays River valley take a well-deserved lunch break.

60 COLUMBIA RIVER

Left top: Giant logs, like this spruce, grew to diameters too large to be handled by conventional log trucks, so more ingenious methods for transporting them were developed.

Left bottom: A train crew momentarily poses by their chunky logging locomotive on the Portland & Southwestern Railroad line owned by Clark and Wilson Lumber Company along the Columbia's south bank.

Right: Logs were yarded from the forest to a "landing" where they were loaded onto railroad cars. This seemingly chaotic mass of cables and wires is a high-lead loading operation using a hayrack boom suspended from the spar tree. This photo was taken during the "high-ball" days of logging when production outweighed all other concerns, including worker safety.

Bottom: The Columbia & Nehalem River Railroad, one of the most extensive logging railroad networks ever operated in the Pacific Northwest, left the Columbia River at Kerry, Oregon, followed the Nehalem River west, and emerged once again at Olney on Youngs River. The Kerry Line, as it was often called, was a common carrier for dozens of individual logging camps, including the Nehalem Timber Company shown here. A number of the camps' buildings are built atop railroad cars so once an area was harvested the camp could be efficiently relocated to the next timber tract.

Left: A bullwhacker keeps a close eye on his five yoke of oxen as they plod along with giant Douglas fir logs in tow over a well-worn skidroad.

Bottom: Tough men and lean bulls.

Right: The machine that changed logging forever: the steam donkey. After relying on human and animal muscle for eons, forest workers began to apply steam power to moving mammoth logs in the late nineteenth century. The innovation sped up the logging industry immensely.

Left: Loggers sought light locomotives with great tractive power to operate on their sometimes-flimsy rail lines. The eleven spot shown is one of the most powerful of all locomotives, the Climax.

Above: All the loggers in Tidewater Timber Company's camp above Young's Bay turned out to have their photo taken on this day. Tidewater's railroad started at the Young's Bay estuary, ran past Olney, and eventually connected to the famed Kerry Line in the Nehalem Valley.

Right: Early logging demanded a great deal of manual labor. Although bull teams were used to skid the logs to tidewater, every other aspect of the operation depended on brute force.

Next spread: Clatskanie, Oregon, a logging hub for decades, looked much like other river towns with waterfront business establishments fixed on countless pilings. A log raft stands by to be towed to market.

Six proud loggers stand on a slice from a spruce log.

Coastal red cedar grew to immense diameters.

The Norwegian-born Simon Benson immigrated to the United States in his teenage years and quickly went about learning the logging trade in the woods of Wisconsin. By his late twenties he had moved west to Oregon and proceeded working his way up through the ranks as an independent logger. By the turn of the twentieth century, Benson owned and operated over a dozen logging camps and six dozen miles of logging railroad. Still, he was keenly interested in entering the booming Southern California lumber market, his only dilemma: uncontrollable freight rates on the one-thousand-mile journey. So, Benson, O.J. Evenson, his business partner, and John Fastabend, an engineering contrac-

tor, began planning the idea for a giant log raft to carry their Oregon timber to California.

The idea was not a new one. In 1894, Captain Hugh Robinson and W.E. Baines had constructed a large cigar-shaped raft on the Columbia River to ship piling to San Francisco on behalf of A.B. Hammond. In fact some thirty-two such rafts had been shipped from the Columbia River before Benson built his first in 1906. The construction of the cigar-raft started by filling a floating cradle that measured 960 feet in length by forty feet wide with tree-length logs by way of a derrick. The long logs served to weave the raft together, creating a more rigid form, to protect it from rough seas. Chains and shackles—roughly 175 tons of them—served to bind the cigar-raft together. The cradle was then removed and hulking steam tugs would arrive to tow the floating giant away. The Benson operation at Wallace Slough, Oregon, built ocean-going rafts year round but only towed them to San Diego during the favorable summer months. From 1906 until World War II, when operations ceased, the Benson concern shipped 116 rafts to California without a single mishap.

The San Diego sawmill combined with the liquidation of much of his timberland made Simon Benson a multimillionaire. Much of his fortune he reinvested in his adopted state. He built the stately Benson Hotel and had twenty bronze drinking fountains installed in downtown Portland. Also in the Rose City, Benson granted a sizable endowment to start Benson Polytechnic High School, one of the Pacific Northwest's leading vocational-technical schools. He also advocated good roads, becoming the first chairman of the Oregon Highway Commission, in addition to planning, supervising, and funding much of the construction of the Columbia River Highway between Portland and Hood River.

Left top: Between 1906 and the 1940s, some 116 Benson sea-going cigar rafts were shipped out of the Columbia River.

Left bottom: During the first half of the twentieth century, the largest things floating on the Columbia River, or in the Pacific Ocean for that matter, were the Benson sea-going log rafts. Many exceeding one thousand feet in length. These mammoth creations carried up to six million board feet of timber to Benson's sawmill in distant San Diego.

Below: The predecessor of Simon Benson's giant sea-going rafts were the Robertson-Baine rafts. The concept for the sea-going rafts came from Nova Scotian Hugh Robertson and was subsequently improved, some even claim perfected, by Simon Benson and associates.

One of the many rags-to-riches stories that originated in the tall timber of the Lower Columbia was that of the Brix brothers—Anton, Albert, Asmus, and Peter. Arriving in the United States in the 1880s, the penniless German immigrants labored to become the owners of sawmills, shipyards, logging firms, and a sizeable towboat concern. This photo shows one of the Brixs' Climax locomotives pulling a massive load of logs at one of their early operations near Knappton, Washington.

Virtually all valleys tributary to the Lower Columbia were crisscrossed with logging railroads, this one in the Deep River, Washington area.

Ezra Meeker who Blazed the first Oregon Trail. 1849.

Left top: Relaxed in his rocking chair, the seasoned settler B.C. Kindred calmly smokes his pipe. Bartholomew Carek Kindred, born in Indiana in 1818, headed west in 1844 and eventually took up residence in what was to become Gearhart. Later, he moved to a farm near the town of Hammond where he and his wife raised twelve children.

Left bottom: Early Pacific Northwest pioneer Ezra Meeker stands as a reminder of the indomitable spirit of the men and women who settled the region. Blessed with longevity, Meeker toured the Northwest giving historic lectures and regaling crowds with his recollections.

Right: W.L. Moody, Knappa's first regular mail carrier, 1917.

Below: Astoria's 1911 centennial celebration continued long into the warm August evening. Besides bands playing in the streets and fireworks rocketing over the river, some twelve-thousand lights were strung throughout downtown as part of the "grand illumination of the city."

Left: Astoria Column, dedicated July 22, 1926, stands as a lone sentinel atop Coxcomb Hill overlooking the Columbia River estuary.

Above: The Columbia River and its tributaries served as the principle means of transportation for centuries before the modern highway systems were completed in the twentieth century. Little launches like the Evangeline *carried goods and passengers from remote backwoods locations to any destination on the river.*

Below: A locomotive and coach of the Astoria & South Coast Railroad cross a drawbridge over an arm of the Columbia River between Goble and Astoria.

Above: Reminiscent of a movie set from the golden age of Hollywood is Henry Tohl's General Merchandise. Born in Germany, Tohl came to America with his parents and after living a couple years in Nebraska moved to the Nehalem Valley, south of Astoria, where he operated a store, hotel, and served as post master.

Below: Hugh A. Robinson, an early barnstormer, arrived in Astoria in August 1911 to demonstrate his Curtis hydroplane as part of the centennial. His manager, megaphone in hand, explained Robinson's aerial exploits as he circled the awestruck grandstands in Uniontown. Although scheduled to do three days of exhibition flights, the show was cut short when Robinson crashed on takeoff on the second day.

Top left: *Dressed in their Sunday best, the passengers of two early touring cars negotiate a switchback on the road between Seaside and Cannon Beach.*

Bottom left: *The river steamer* General Washington *departs Deep River, Washington, which, in its heyday, featured a hotel, saloon, two stores, multiple warehouses, and a movie house. A constant flow of men, goods, and logs came through little towns like Deep River thanks to the logging camps located in the hills above.*

Top right: *Sherman & Ward Livery & Sale Stables and* The Astorian *office along Commercial Street in downtown Astoria around the turn of the twentieth century.*

Bottom right: *Traveling salesmen worked hard to peddle their wares in the hinterland communities of the Lower Columbia.*

Left: To celebrate their Norse heritage the Scandinavian community of Astoria sponsored a weeklong centennial celebration in April 1911. Horse-drawn floats adorned their large parade through downtown including this extravagant Viking ship.

Below: Scantily-clad vixens serve crab cockails to an interested crowd on the Astoria waterfront in the post-World War II era.

Right top: The Astoria Regatta's celebrated water sports events included all sorts of races from half-pint speedboats to sailing boats to gillnet boats. Originated in the early 1890s, the Regatta is considered by many to be the oldest festival in the Pacific Northwest.

Right Bottom: Sailing boats, pleasure craft, fishing boats— everybody took to the water during Astoria's annual regatta. The Astoria Regatta, started in 1894, was one of the finest watersports carnivals in the region. A salmon derby with cash prizes.

Top left: The Georgie Lou *and other pleasure craft cruise the* Columbia *during Astoria's annual regatta.*

Bottom left: Nearly thirty blocks of downtown Astoria lay in ruin December 1922. Miraculously, only one person died, that being a car salesman who suffered a heart attack while attempting to push automobiles off his burning car lot.

Right: One of the few survivors of the Astoria fire of 1922 was the Bank of Commerce's vault. Not a bad advertisement for The Mosler Safe Company.

Below: Two sentries of the Oregon National Guard stand guard amidst the smoking rubble in order to keep order and prevent looting.

Left: After the devastating fire of 1922, Astoria set about rebuilding its downtown business district. Some of the new stone buildings exhibited a sense of panache, like the Liberty Theatre with its distinct streetside colonnade.

Top right: In 1966, with the completion of the Astoria-Megler Bridge, Oregon and Washington were finally linked by a roadway near the river's mouth. The bridge brought an end to long-running ferry service in the area.

Bottom right: Moth Balls. After the cessation of hostilities in the Pacific Ocean following World War II, hundreds of mothballed liberty ships and LSTs were brought to Tongue Point upriver from Astoria to be scrapped.

Footnotes

1 Rick Rubin, *Naked Against the Rain: The People of the Lower Columbia River*, 1770-
1830, Portland, OR: Far Shore Press, 1999, p. 143.

2 John Scofield, *Hail Columbia: Robert Gray, John Kendrick, and the Pacific Fur Trade*,
Portland, OR: Oregon Historical Society Press, 1993, pp. 341-342.

3 Rubin, *Naked Against the Rain*, pp. 200-201.

4 Rubin, *Naked Against the Rain*, p. 344.

5 John Kirk Townsend, *Narrative of a Journey across the Rocky Mountains, to the Columbia
River, and a Visit to the Sandwich Islands*, Chili, &c., with a Scientific Appendix,
Corvallis, OR: Oregon State University Press, 1999 (1839), p. 132.

6 Alfred A. Cleveland, "Social and Economic History of Astoria," *Oregon Historical
Quarterly*, Volume IV, No. 2, June 1903, p. 136.

7 James G. Swan. *The Northwest Coast: Or, Three Years' Residence in Washington
Territory*, Seattle: University of Washington Press, 1972 (1857), pp. 104, 107.

8 Carlton E. Appelo, Altoona, Wahkiakum County, Ilwaco, WA: Pacific Printing Company,
1984 (1972), p. 8.

9 Hummasti, P.G. "Ethnicity and Radicalism: The Finns of Astoria and the Toveri, 1890-
1930." *Oregon Historical Quarterly*, Vol. 96, No. 4, Winter 1995-96, p. 366.

10 Ed Niska, "Astoria's 'Union Fish'," *Cumtux*, Volume 8, No. 2, Spring 1988, p. 34. Also
see Cynthia J. Marconeri, "Chinese-Americans in Astoria, Oregon, 1880-1930,"
Cumtux, Volume 13, No. 3, Summer 1993, pp. 31-37.

11 In 1880, some $7,300 of the Astoria's $20,800 in revenue was raised via liquor license
fees. "Astoria: On The Wild Side," *Cumtux*, Vol. 12, No. 3, Summer 1992, p. 40.

12 Denise Alborn, "Shanghai Days In Astoria," *Cumtux*, Volume 9, No. 1, Winter 1988, p. 13.

13 Rebecca Rubens, "The Pioneer Trullingers," *Cumtux*, Volume 9, No. 2, Spring 1989, p. 12.

14 Carlos Arnaldo Schwantes, *Columbia River: Gateway to the West*, Moscow, ID:
University of Idaho Press, 2000, p. 47.

15 Hubert Howe Bancroft, The Works of Hubert Howe Bancroft, Volume XXX, *History of
Oregon*, Volume II, 1848-1888, San Francisco: The History Company, Publishers, 1888, p. 758.

16 Messages of the Governors of the Territory of Washington, to the Legislative Assembly,
1854-1889, Charles M. Gates (editor), Seattle: University of Washington Press, 1940, p. 272.

17 "Alfred E. Houchen," *Sou'wester*, Volume XX, No. 3, Autumn 1985.

18 Roger T. Tetlow, "Peter Dorcich's Record Catch," *Cumtux*, Volume 4, No. 3, Summer
1984, p. 15.

19 "The Frankfort Chronicle," compiled by Skamokawa Community Library, *Sou'wester*,
Volume XIV, No. 2, Summer 1984, p. 27.

20 "Big Flag Pole Fell with Crash," *Astoria Daily Budget*, July 28, 1911, p. 1 and <u>Astoria
Daily Budget</u>, June 5, 1914, p. 6.

21 "Thousands Saw Robinson Fly," *Astoria Daily Budget*, August 24, 1911.

22 Walter Mattila, "Memories of the Astoria Fire—1922," *Cumtux*, Volume 5, No. 2, Spring
1985, p. 29.

Photograph identification

Copies of these photographs can be
ordered in convenient sizes by con-
tacting The Compleat Photographer,
475 14th St., Astoria, OR 97103.
503-325-0759
www.compleatphotographer.com

Page 1: 135c8, TCP.02
Page 4: 15-10-00-1 TCP.03
Page 5: 117, TCP.02
Page 6: 554, TCP.03
Page 7: 10-66-10-1, TCP.02
Page 9-8: 147
Page 10: 875, TCP.03
Page 13: 01-46-00-1, TCP.02
Page 17: 295, TCP.02
Page 18: 280, TCP.02
Page 20: 15-49-00-02, TCP.02
Page 23: 20-31-00-3, TCP.03
Page 24: 01-50-89-1, TCP.03
Page 25: 07-42-06-01, TCP.03
Page 27: 01-83-98-1, TCP.03
Page 28-29: 07-76-15-03. TCP.03
Page 30: 574
Page 31: 75-22-017, TCP.03
Page 32-33: 31-10-00-01
Page 34: top: 551, TCP.02 bottom:
15-76-00-01, TCP.03
Page 35: A119 TCP.03
Page 36: 14-12-7-1 TCP.03
Page 37: top: 14-12-07-2, TCP.02
bottom: 21-12-06-0, TCP.03
Page 38: 135N "5" or 5x7 NEG.
534-21
Page 39: 556, TCP.02
Page 40: top: 814, TCP.03 bottom:
267/081295-1, TCP.02
Page 41: top: 08-12-09-01, TCP.03
bottom: 08-12-09-03, TCP.03
Page 42: 21-12-06-9, TCP.03
Page 43: top: 135c13, TCP.02 bot-
tom: 16-12-07-1, TCP.03
Page 44: top 31-18-991, TCP.03
bottom: 21-12-06-02, TCP.02
Page 45: 01-15-15-02, TCP.03
Page 46: top: 281 bottom: 01-15-20-
02, TCP.03
Page 47: 402-5135N 39A, TCP.03
Page 48-49: 15-45-00-1
Page 50: top: 135H22, TCP.02 bot-
tom: 135B27, TCP.02
Page 51: top: S135 neg#7 original
#534 bottom: #1008, TCP.03

FURTHER READINGS

Page 52: top: 15-45-00-02, TCP.02 bottom right: 143 21-1, TCP.03 bottom left: 194, TCP.02
Page 53: top: 536, TCP.02 bottom: 568, TCP.02
Page 54: top: 01-43-001, TCP.02 bottom: 06-42-00-1, TCP.03
Page 55: 2031-005, TCP.03
Page 56: top: 20-31-00-1, TCP.03 bottom: 538, TCP.03
Page 57: top: 21-30-35-1, TCP.03
Page 58-59: 20-31-00-2
Page 60: top: 987, TCP.03 bottom: #143307, TCP.03
Page 61: top: 14-35-07-3, TCP.03 bottom: 14-32-07-1, TCP.03
Page 62: top: 20-36-89-1, TCP.03 bottom: 20-36-00-1, TCP.03
Page 63: 20-34-00-1, TCP.03
Page 64: top: 03-33-16-1, TCP.03 bottom: 23-33-00-02, TCP.03
Page 65: top: 20-33-00-4, TCP.03 bottom: 14-36-64-1, TCP.03
Page 66-67: 23-18-18-01, TCP.03
Page 68: 20-30-00-01
Page 69: 20-31-00-4
Page 70: top: #135 NEG "5" original 5x7 #537.23
Page 71: 129, TCP.03
Page 72: 182, TCP.03
Page 73: 894 5135N 41A, TCP.03
Page 74: top: 456, TCP.02 bottom: 563, TCP.03
Page 75: top: 03-65-17-1, TCP.03 bottom: 992A, TCP.03
Page 76: top left: 575 TCP.02 top right: 796, TCP.03 bottom: 562, TCP.03
Page 77: top: 03-53-00-1, TCP.02 bottom: #1028, TCP.03
Page 78: top: 11-96-10-01, TCP.02 bottom: 548, TCP.03
Page 79: top: 01-63-00-1, TCP.03 bottom: 20-67-00-1, TCP.02
Page 80: top:01-72-11-3, TCP.03 bottom: 131, TCP.02
Page 81: top: N135 S26 146, TCP.03 bottom: 135N 528 210, TCP.03
Page 82: top: 135N S29 208, TCP.03 bottom: 1-75-22-15, TCP.03
Page 83: top: A116, TCP.03 bottom: 75-22-00-6, TCP.03
Page 84: A1, TCP.03
Page 85: top: 01-85-66-1, TCP.03 bottom: 24-26-44-1, TCP.02

Appelo, Carlton. Altoona, Wahkiakum County, Washington. Ilwaco, WA: Pacific Printing Company, 1972. Appelo, one of the most noted north-bank historians, has written a number of comprehensive histories on southwestern Washington's fishing and logging communities ,including Brookfield (1966), Cottardi (1980), Deep River (1978), Knappton (1975), and Pillar Rock (1969).

Gibbs, James A. *Pacific Graveyard: A Narrative of Shipwrecks where the Columbia River Meets the Pacific Ocean.* Portland, OR: Binford & Mort Publishing, 1953. An old hand at nautical history, Gibbs gives factual accounts of virtually every shipwreck to occur between Clatsop Spit and Willapa Bay.

Holbrook, Stewart H. *The Columbia.* New York: Rinehart and Company, Inc., 1956. Holbrook's popular account of the Columbia is an absorbing overview of the entire river. Although he passed away in 1964, Holbrook is remembered as the Northwest's best story-teller and *The Columbia* exhibits his pension for writing.

Martin, Irene. *Legacy and Testament: The Story of Columbia River Gillnetters.* Pullman, WA: Washington State University, 1994. Martin tells the history of the Columbia River gill-netter with a personal assurance, because besides being Wahkiakum County's foremost historian, Irene and her husband Kent are commercial fishermen.

Rubin, Rick. *Naked Against the Rain: The People of the Lower Columbia River,* 1770-1830. Portland, OR: Far Shore Press, 1999. This recent account comes from the Portland-based free-lance writer who is one of the foremost experts on the people who first lived on the Columbia River. It is both well documented and written.

Schwantes, Carlos Arnaldo. *Columbia River: Gateway to the West.* Moscow, ID: University of Idaho Press, 2000. A history professor and avid photographer, Schwantes has combined a stirring overview of the river with incredible color images in this handsome monograph.

Tetlow, Roger T. and Graham H. Barbey. Barbey, *The Story of a Pioneer Columbia River Salmon Packer.* Portland, OR: Binford & Mort Publishing, 1990. An interesting account of the Columbia River's salmon canning industry is wrapped around this biography of salmon cannery operator Henry Barbey.

Ziak, Rex. *In Full View.* Astoria, OR: Moffitt House Publishing, 2002. Years of research and on-the-ground exploration are at the core of this narrative on Lewis and Clark, complemented by an array of exquisite color photographs.

More Outdoor
Appreciation Books

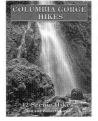

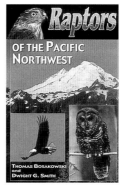